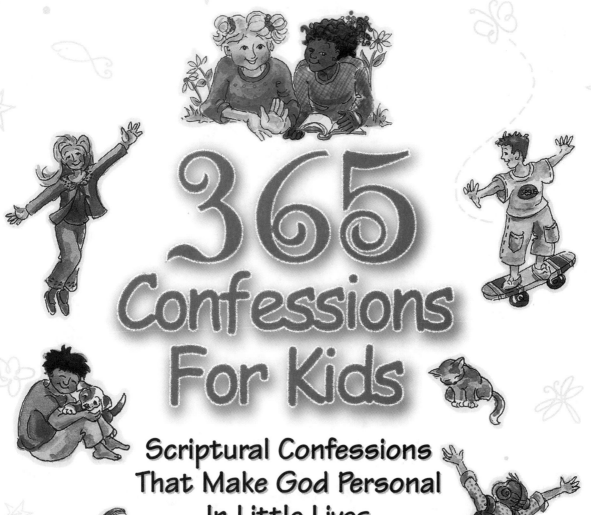

365
Confessions
For Kids

Scriptural Confessions That Make God Personal In Little Lives

Virginia Kite

Presented to

_____

on the occasion of

_____

By _____

Date _____

Jesus • Love • Forgive • Share • Savior • Peace

365 Confessions For Kid's
Scriptural Confessions That Make God Personal In Little Lives
ISBN 1-57794-347-3
Copyright © 2001 by Virginia Kite
P.O. Box 33110
Tulsa, Oklahoma 74153

Published by Harrison House, Inc.
P.O. Box 35035
Tulsa, Oklahoma 74153

Foreword: Why Confessions?

Faith comes by *hearing and hearing* the Word of God. If a man believes in his heart and *confesses* with his mouth the Lord Jesus, he shall be saved. Whoever shall speak to the mountain shall have whatever he says. (See Rom. 10:17; Rom. 10:9 and Mark 11:23.)

God intended for man to live by His Word. He gave us from earliest times a written record of His teachings—the Bible—and He has preserved it over the centuries. He clearly intended that we hear and learn and speak His living Word.

Man *is* what he believes, and he *becomes* what he confesses. When belief is weak, confession can make it stronger. Hearing the Word develops faith. Faith overcomes the weakness of the flesh.

Speaking the Word puts the devil on the run. When tempted by Satan in the wilderness, Jesus did what He now expects us to do: He used the Word of God coming through His own lips and verbally drove the devil off!

Teach your kids to pray daily. Teach them to read God's Word daily. And teach them how to use their spiritual authority by speaking God's Word daily over all situations. God's Word never fails!

So shall My Word be that goes forth from
My mouth; it shall not return to Me void,
but it shall accomplish what I please, and
it shall prosper in the thing for which I sent it.

Isaiah 55:11

How To Use This Book

A Scripture confession is powerful. This book is loaded with *God's Power!*

The 365 confessions in this book can be used either by date reference, or by number reference. They are ordered by date for the convenience of those who like to have a dated devotional. But please don't limit the book by beginning only on January 1! It can be started any day of the year!

If you obtain the book in July, you can begin the child's daily confessions either with the date "July 1," or with the numerical sequence beginning with "Day 1."

The confessions are also listed in a subject index in the back of the book. There will be many times you will want to recall a certain Scripture, or have need of God's insight into a specific area. With the index, you will easily locate the Scripture(s) you need.

The confessions can be used in the mornings to begin the day. They can be used to wind up early morning prayer or to precede or follow Bible story time at night. They can even be used by the entire family as a short but dynamic group confession before the evening meal is shared together.

Appropriate Scriptures and confessions can be used over and over. They can be taped to the mirror or recorded on the cassette player to minister to a specific area of need in a child. I have had successful experience in recording certain Scripture confessions and replaying them during the night on an auto-reverse tape player. The child's subconscious has been found to be a definite avenue by which he can receive positive reinforcement from God's Word.

This book is intended to be used by parent and child together. It should prove to be a fun activity which both child and parent will look forward to each day! The Scripture reference can be read to the child, or a brief paraphrase given of the Scripture, depending upon the child's age. Then, the confession should be read to the child, phrase by phrase, so the child can easily repeat after you. *Use expression and emphasis so that the meaning can be grasped fully. Concentrate on the child's understanding and enjoying the confession. If he "really gets into it," it will get into him!*

Lastly, be assured that, whether Scripture is "straight from the Bible" or paraphrased into kids' language, it is God's Word, and God's Word works!

The Story of the Bible

God made the earth for people to enjoy. He wanted it to be a good and perfect and beautiful place for His people to live. He wanted to be a loving Father to every person. But the people that God had created sinned. When they chose to obey the devil, they let trouble come into the earth.

God is a good God! But the devil is a bad devil. The devil brought sin, sickness, poverty and pain into the earth. Every evil thing is from the devil.

God's heart was broken. But, because He loved His people so much, He had a plan.

Jesus, God's Son, lived with Him in heaven. All things that were made were spoken into being by Jesus. Jesus loved the people that He and His Father God had made.

The plan was: God would let Jesus come to earth and live as a man. He would show the people how much God loved them.

Then Jesus would have to die. He would take all the sins and sicknesses and sorrows of the people upon Himself.

When Jesus died on the cross, for a little while the devil thought he had won. But God had a BIG surprise for him!

God raised Jesus from the dead! He was alive again! The devil's plan was defeated! Through Jesus' dying and rising again, God could get His people back!

Now God's people could have power over the devil again. All they needed to do was accept Jesus as Lord and use His Word and His Name to overcome the devil!

There was hope again for the people of God! They could have a victorious life on earth and an eternal life with God and Jesus! God would be the Father He had planned to be. And we—those who believe—would be His children!

This is the story of the Bible.
This is the story of God's love for mankind.

January 1

*All your children shall be taught
by the Lord, and great shall be
the peace of your children.*

Isaiah 54:18

I am a child of God!
I am taught by God's Word.
I KEEP His Word in my heart!
The Word of God GUIDES my life.
I am HAPPY and BLESSED!
I have no cares, no fears and no worries.
I am full of GOD'S PEACE.
God's Word is doing great things in my life!

January 2

*...That you may become blameless and harmless,
children of God without fault in the midst
of a crooked and perverse generation,
among whom you shine as lights in the world.*

Philippians 2:15

Jesus is my LIGHT and His light is in me!
I will live my life as a child of God should live.
I will remember that Jesus needs me!
I am an EXAMPLE of HIS goodness and love.
I AM A LIGHT THAT SHINES even when darkness is around.
People will see my light and be led to Jesus!

January 3

"Let the little children come to Me, and do not
forbid them for of such is the kingdom of God."
And He took them up in His arms, put
His hands on them, and blessed them.

Mark 10:14,16

3

Jesus, Your Word tells me how much You love me!
YOU WANTED little children to come to You!
You didn't push them away. You hugged and blessed them!
I'm so glad You love me, Lord!
I FEEL YOUR PRESENCE! I FEEL YOUR LOVE!
I know I can always trust You!
I LOVE YOU, JESUS!

January 4

I will praise You, for I am fearfully and wonderfully made.

Psalm 139:14

4

Thank you, Father, for the BODY You gave me.
Thank You for making me just the way I am!
I'll take GOOD CARE of my body. I'll eat good foods,
dress wisely, exercise diligently and rest properly.
In Jesus' name I resist anything that would hurt my body!
Thank You, Father, for Your wisdom and Your protection for the body I live in!

January 5

For whom He foreknow, He also predestinated
to be conformed to the image of His Son, that
He might be the firstborn among many brethren.

Romans 8:29

God has a SPECIAL calling on my life!
Before I was born, God knew I would want to serve Him!
I ACCEPT GOD'S CALLING. I will obey the Lord!
My life will bring glory to the name of Jesus!
I choose to walk in God's perfect will.
I will be faithful to the trust HE has in ME!

January 6

Rejoice in the Lord always. Again I will say, rejoice!

Philippians 4:4

JESUS MAKES ME GLAD!
Every day I am full of JOY and STRENGTH!
I praise God in the morning!
I sing songs to Him!
I let Him know I love Him!
When night comes, I am full of peace.
I dream happy dreams!
I don't let sadness come into my heart.
I am happy, happy, happy in my Lord!

January 7

There is therefore now no condemnation to those who are in Christ Jesus, who do not walk according to the flesh, but according to the Spirit.

Romans 8:1

Father, it's so good to know that I AM YOUR CHILD!
You ALWAYS love me! Even when I sin, You love me.
The devil makes me feel guilty and bad.
But You forgive me and make me feel glad!
Nothing can ever separate me from Your love!
I'm growing STRONG in my spirit!
I'll keep right on serving You, in Jesus' name!

January 8

He who is slow to wrath has great understanding.

Proverbs 14:29

I am not a pouter!
The peace of God's Spirit is in me.
I keep my temper under control!
I am kind. I am loving. I am understanding!
If I do get angry, I get over it QUICKLY!
I FORGIVE AND FORGET wrongs done to me.
I'm learning to think like Jesus!
I walk in the love of Jesus!

January 9

I will delight myself in Your statutes;
I will not forget Your Word.

Psalm 119:16

9

I'm learning MORE OF GOD'S WORD each day!
I read my Bible or listen to others read to me.
God's Word is shaping my life!
I will USE God's Word to make friends.
His Word will SHOW me how to treat others.
His Word will help me to make
EVERY DAY A DAY OF BLESSINGS!

January 10

(If) you pay attention to the one wearing the
fine clothes and say to him, "You sit here in
a good place," and say to the poor man, "You stand
there,"...have you not shown partiality among yourselves.

James 2:3,4

10

Sometimes a new child comes into our neighborhood, school or church.
They may feel lonely or left out.
I won't mind if the new person is rich or poor.
It doesn't matter what they wear.
I don't care what color their skin is.
The most important thing is, do they know Jesus?
I will SHOW THEM GOD'S LOVE.

January 19

19

"Take heed that you do not despise one of these little ones, for I say to you that in heaven their angels always see the face of My Father who is in heaven."

Matthew 18:10

Angels are God's MIGHTY servants.
They travel to and from heaven and earth.
They are sent to protect GOD'S PEOPLE!
Children have guardian angels
that watch over them all their lives.
WHEN I PRAY TO GOD AND SPEAK GOD'S WORD
IN FAITH, THE ANGELS GET BUSY!
They see to it that the Word of God is performed!
Thank You, Lord, for Your power, Your Word
and Your angels watching over me!

January 20

20

But whoever listens to me will dwell safely, and will be secure, without fear of evil.

Proverbs 1:33

Thank You, Lord, that You are always with me.
I AM NEVER ALONE.
I walk with You and talk with You.
In Your presence I have no fear!
No evil can overtake me, in Jesus' name!

January 21

*And whatever we ask we receive from Him,
because we keep His commandments and
do those things that are pleasing in His sight.*

1 John 3:22

God hears my prayers!
He is always listening to me!
He hears me because I am His very own child.
He answers my prayers because
I am not selfish when I pray.
When I obey His commandments,
He is pleased to give me the desires of my heart.

January 22

*The steps of a good man are ordered by the Lord,
and He delights in his way. The law of his God
is in his heart; none of his steps shall slide.*

Psalm 37:23,31

My steps are ordered by the Lord!
God will guide me all the days of my life.
The Lord will lead me to the right places
at the right times. He will give me godly friends.
God will lead me to the right person to marry.
I choose to follow Jesus! He will show me
God's perfect plan for my life!

January 23

"Whoever comes to Me, and hears my sayings and does them...is like a man building a house, who dug deep and laid the foundation on the rock."

Luke 6:47

I'm building my house on the solid rock!
I'm digging deep into GOD'S WORD.
God's Word is a Rock that can't be moved!
No matter what happens—
floods, winds, earthquakes, evil in the world—
nothing can shake my faith in God's Word!
God's Word will remain forever!
His Truth will be my strength and my victory!

January 24

Sing praises to the Lord,
who dwells in Zion!
Declare His deeds among the people.

Psalm 9:11

Lord Jesus,
I will sing praises to You forever!
You are my very good Friend!
You give me joy, joy, joy in my heart!
You fill me with your wisdom and knowledge.
You turn my problems into victories!
I worship and adore You, Jesus.

January 25

So let each one give as he purposes in
his heart, not grudgingly or of necessity;
for God loves a cheerful giver.

2 Corinthians 9:7

I am a cheerful giver! I am not selfish!
My money, my clothes, my toys are all from God.
I'm thankful for all the nice things I have!
God has blessed me, so I love to bless others!
Sharing my blessings shows people that God
cares about them. I become God's HELPER!
My heart delights in giving!

January 26

Let another man praise you, and not your own mouth...

Proverbs 27:2

God made me special. There's just one me!
He gave me gifts, talents and abilities.
I can be a blessing to many people!
I give thanks and honor to God for my talents!
All that I have comes from Him!
I'll not be proud or brag about what I can do.
I'll remember that God expects me to bless others
with the blessings He has given me!

January 27

Finally, my brethren, be strong in the Lord and in the power of His might. Put on the whole armor of God, that you may be able to stand against the wiles of the devil.

Ephesians 6:10,11

I begin each day putting on my ARMOR OF GOD!
When I'm wearing God's clothes,
I know I'll have a great day!
The devil will be scared to pieces!
He may try to put up a fight...But
I'll just keep standing tall in God's armor
UNTIL I WIN!

This is the armor of God I wear!
The HELMET OF SALVATION covers my head.
It protects my mind from confusion.
The BREASTPLATE OF RIGHTEOUSNESS covers my heart.
Because of Jesus shedding His blood for me,
I am holy to God.
The BELT OF TRUTH is around my waist.
My life is guided by God's truth!
GOSPEL SHOES are on my feet!
Everywhere I go, I tell God's GOOD NEWS!
I carry the SHIELD OF FAITH in my hand.
My faith causes God's Word to work.
My faith puts the devil on the run!
The SWORD OF THE SPIRIT is in my other hand.
The mighty Word of God cuts through every problem!
I keep my armor polished and shining with PRAYER!
Prayer surrounds myself and others with God's
POWER all through the day!

January 29

"And whenever you stand praying, if you have anything against anyone, forgive him that your Father in heaven may also forgive you your trespasses."

Mark 11:25

I am a forgiver!
Someone I love may yell at me, but I'll understand
that they didn't mean to. I'll forgive.
A friend of mine may hurt my feelings,
but I'll walk in love. I'll forgive.
Right now, I make a decision to
forgive any wrong that has ever been done to me.
I receive total healing of all hurt.
I will always strive to be slow to get angry
and quick to forgive!

January 30

If there is any virtue and if there is anything praiseworthy—meditate on these things.

Philippians 4:8

Jesus, I need Your help to stay pure.
Some music is not good for my ears to hear.
Many movies and TV shows shouldn't be seen by God's kids.
Help me to be wise! Make me strong so I can say NO
to anything that's not good in Your sight. With Your
help, I choose what is good and resist what is bad!

January 31

All Scripture is given by inspiration of God, and is profitable for doctrine, for reproof, for correction, for instruction in righteousness, that the man of God may be complete, thoroughly equipped for every good work.

2 Timothy 3:16,17

I am equipped for every good work!
God's Word is teaching me everything I need
to know to be a soldier in His army.
I have the Spirit of God in me!
I have God's armor on!
I have guardian angels surrounding me!
I have God's ability growing on the inside of me!
I pray, speak and live in God's grace,
God's love and God's authority.
He has equipped me to win!

31

February 1

When you lie down, you will not be afraid;
yes, you will lie down and your sleep will be sweet.

Proverbs 3:24

Now I lay me down to sleep...
And when I dream, they'll all be sweet!
Thank You, Jesus, for good, peaceful rest at night.
Thank You that You are always awake, watching over me.
Thank You for my guardian angel protecting me.
I am never afraid.
I don't mind the dark.
There's nothing to be afraid of
since You're around!
So-o-o-o,
I will close my eyes
and have happy dreams.
Good night, Jesus.
I love you.

February 2

Giving thanks always for all things to God
the Father in the name of our Lord Jesus Christ.

Ephesians 5:20

Father,
Thank You, Thank You, Thank You
for all the wonderful things You give me!
You fill me up with JOY!
I have no fear because You give me FAITH!
You've given me a nice, safe place to live.
I have a family to love me.
ALL my needs are met!
I appreciate Your goodness to me.
Thank You, heavenly Father!

February 3

Be anxious for nothing, but in everything by
prayer and supplication, with thanksgiving,
let your requests be made known to God.

Philippians 4:6

I resist the spirit of WORRY in Jesus' name!
I have no cares! I am GOD'S child! He meets my needs!
He keeps me safe. I am blessed in all I do.
When I pray, God hears my prayers.
I thank God always, because He never lets me down!

February 4

He who guards his mouth preserves his life...
A righteous man hates lying.

Proverbs 13:3,5a

I will guard my mouth.
I hate lies; so I don't tell them!
Lord, You always tell the truth, so I trust and believe You. Because
I tell the truth, people will trust and believe me.
In Jesus' name, I resist temptations to lie!
I receive God's quality of truthfulness in my life.

February 5

Let your gentleness be known to all men.

Philippians 4:5

Lord, You are gentle and kind.
You live in me, so I am gentle and kind, too.
I watch out for children who are smaller than me.
I am thoughtful of my classmates at school.
I speak cheerful and uplifting words.
I am polite and helpful to older people.
By my gentleness I show others the love of God.

February 6

Let us not become conceited, provoking one another, envying one another.

Galatians 5:26

I am not proud or conceited.
I have a humble spirit.
My ways are gentle.
I do not criticize others.
I'm not bossy!
I don't cause others to get angry with me.
I show God's love to everyone.
I am always ready to be a true friend.

February 7

For your obedience has become known to all.

Romans 16:19

Lord,
I know YOU are watching me all the time.
The Bible says PEOPLE are watching me, too!
People around me will see JESUS in me.
They will see that I OBEY You.
They will see me LISTENING to my parents and teachers.
Because I obey, I am a GOOD example to others!
Thank You, Holy Spirit, for HELPING me to obey!

February 8

39

If you are reproached for the name of Christ, blessed
are you, for the Spirit of glory and of God rests upon you...

1 Peter 4:14

If anyone rejects me
because I love Jesus,
I'll still be happy.
I'll stand up for my Lord!
People who think they don't need Jesus will find out
that living for the devil just makes them a loser.
When they decide they want to be a winner,
I'll have the answer for them: JESUS!

February 9

40

Behold what manner of love the Father has bestowed
on us, that we should be called children of God!

1 John 3:1

Father,
What love You have for me!
Because I accepted Your Son, Jesus,
You accepted me as Your child!
You became my very own Father!
You love me just the same as You love Jesus!
I will never have anything to worry about, because the God of
heaven and earth is MY FATHER!

February 10

Let nothing be done through
selfish ambition or conceit, but
in lowliness of mind let each esteem
others better than himself.

Philippians 2:3

I set a goal to love others as much as I love myself!
I will try to think how other people feel.
I won't criticize or make fun of anyone.
God made us all. He loves each of us the same.
He wants everyone to get along with each other.
I will do my best to look through God's eyes,
and see every person as valuable and precious.

February 11

"You shall rise before the gray headed and
honor the presence of an old man and
fear your God: I am the Lord."

Leviticus 19:32

God is pleased because I respect my elders.
I am polite to grown-ups. I say "Yes, Sir," and "Yes, Ma'am."
I am courteous. I open doors for older people.
I pick up things they drop.
I listen to the wisdom that older people have.
I don't interrupt. I'm patient and quiet.
I learn a lot from those who know more than I do.
Thank You, Lord, for putting wonderful grown-ups
into my life to teach me.

March 20

For I am not ashamed of the gospel of Christ, for it is
the power of God to salvation for everyone who believes...

Romans 1:16

79

The gospel is GOD'S GOOD NEWS!
The gospel is Jesus coming to earth to save me!
God let Jesus come to die for my sins.
But the GOOD news is that Jesus rose again!
He whipped the devil! He did it so I could be
saved from the devil running my life!
I don't have to be sick, poor or defeated!
I am a winner because of God's good news!

March 21

But without faith it is impossible to please Him,
for he who comes to God must believe that He is, and
that He is a rewarder of those who diligently seek Him.

Hebrews 11:6

80

God is happy when I use my faith!
FAITH simply means that I BELIEVE GOD.
Faith says, "I believe God's Word is true,
and I depend on it." Faith says, "God is good!
He has rewards for me when I put Him first!"
Thank You, Lord, for helping me to grow STRONG IN FAITH!

March 22

The plans of the diligent lead
surely to plenty.

Proverbs 21:5

If I work hard, I can get lots more things done.
I can help Mom and Dad and still have time to play!
I can work hard at school lessons, and learn
things that will help me all my life!
I can work diligently to obey God's Word
and do my part to change the world!
I'm a worker and not a loafer, in Jesus' name!

March 23

He sent His Word and healed them.

Psalm 107:20

There is healing in God's Word.
When I speak God's Word, I grow stronger.
When I hear God's Word, sickness has to flee.
Disease and infection run out the door!
Health comes because God's Word works in my body!
I walk in health and strength, in Jesus' name!

March 24

Be sober, be vigilant; because your adversary
the devil walks about like a roaring lion, seeking
whom he may devour. Resist him, steadfast in the faith!

1 Peter 5:8,9

God is on my side! God has an enemy named Satan.
Because I belong to God, Satan is my enemy, too.
The devil looks for ways to bring trouble to me.
But I resist him!
I have extra power from God's Holy Spirit!
God's ability is on the inside of me!
God and I together will put the enemy on the run!

March 25

The angel of the Lord encamps all around
those who fear Him, and delivers them.

Psalm 34:7

Heavenly Father,
Thank You for putting angels all around me.
I can't see the angels with my natural eyes,
but Your Word says they are watching over me.
They have a job to do. They help You protect me!
They keep evil away from me!
I will be obedient to You, Father,
so the angels will be able to
do their job!

March 26

Do not love the world or the things in
the world. If anyone loves the world,
the love of the Father is not in him.

1 John 2:15

My heart belongs to Jesus!
He is my first love!
I don't love the things of the world
or the things money can buy.
I enjoy all the blessings God gives me,
but I don't live to receive...
I live to give. I live to love.
My goal is to live forever with Jesus and
to show others that they can, too!

March 27

An excellent wife is the crown of her husband.

Proverbs 12:4

I'm not too young to claim just the right person to marry.
God is already working on my future mate!
He's preparing someone wonderful to share my life with me.
A joyful person who loves Jesus is on the way!
We will have a loving marriage and family.
God will be the center of our home.
Thank You, Jesus, for preparing us to be together!

March 28

*Bring all the tithes into the storehouse,
that there may be food in My house.*

Malachi 3:10a

I am a tither!
I joyfully give back to God one tenth of all
the money He sends to me.
One tenth of my allowance belongs to God.
One tenth of the money I earn goes back to God.
I am so blessed I want to give MORE than a tenth!
Giving to God is one way of saying,
"Thank You, Father, for all You've given to me."
GIVING TO GOD TELLS HIM I LOVE HIM!

March 29
2 Peter 1:2-8 (Personalized)

I walk in God's grace.
I am filled with His peace.
I am rich with His blessings.
He has given me all things I need
to live a happy and godly life.
He has given me the keys to His own divine nature.
I am growing in faith,
virtue, knowledge and self-control.
I am increasing in perseverance,
godliness, brotherly kindness and love.
I am becoming faithful in the knowledge
of my Lord Jesus Christ.

April 10

Make a joyful shout to the Lord, all you lands!

Psalm 100:1

100

I will shout to the Lord with joy!
I serve my Lord with gladness.
I come into His presence with singing.
I remember that God made me and I am His!
I enter His gates with thanksgiving.
I praise Him and bless His holy name!
For the Lord is good.
His mercy is everlasting!
His truth shall bless all generations!

April 11

Obey those who rule over you, and be submissive,
for they watch out for your souls, as those
who must give account.

Hebrews 13:17

101

I obey those God has placed over me: my parents,
my teachers, my pastor. All of these people have
a BIG responsibility. God told them to watch out for
my soul! God told them to teach me and train me.
I listen to my elders with respect. I learn with joy.
I have a cheerful attitude, and an obedient heart.
The angels will be keeping good heavenly records on me!

April 12
God is love.

1 John 4:8b

God loves me! He calls me His BELOVED.
He says I am the APPLE OF HIS EYE!
He loves me with an EVERLASTING LOVE.
His love will NEVER FAIL.
He will NEVER LEAVE ME NOR FORSAKE ME.
I'm HIS LITTLE CHILD.
He's MY LOVING FATHER.
GOD'S LOVE WILL SURROUND ME FOREVER!

April 13
This is the day which the Lord has made we will rejoice and be glad in it.

Psalm 118:24

Thank You, Jesus,
for another day of Your goodness and love!
This will be a day of learning and growing.
I call this day blessed!
I will do my best to make it a happy day.
I will be glad and rejoice!
My heart will sing with joy!
I will spread joy to others all around me!

April 14

My son, do not forget my law, but let your heart keep my commands; for length of days and long life and peace they will add to you.

Proverbs 3:1,2

My Bible is a treasure that I cherish.
I love God's Word because I know He's talking to me!
I do my best to listen to God and live by His Word.
I will have a long, healthy life
because God's Word is working in me!
I'll have peace and joy no matter what,
because His Word keeps my faith strong!

April 15

"Peace I leave with you, My peace I give to you; not as the world gives do I give to you. Let not your heart be troubled, neither let it be afraid."

John 14:27

Dear Lord,
No matter what happens around me—in my family, or in school, or in the world—I will always be filled with Your peace. My heart will not be troubled or afraid.
You will always be able to work things out,
because my faith is working! I walk in faith, not fear!
THE PEACE YOU GIVE controls my feelings!

April 16

Therefore we do not lose heart.
Even though our outward man is perishing,
yet the inward man is being renewed day by day.

2 Corinthians 4:16

I am not discouraged. I am full of hope!
My hope is in my God! He makes all things good.
He fixes things that go wrong. My heart is full of joy
because I trust in Him. My spirit is lively and strong!
My inner man will stand up tall and shout,
"Hallelujah! Nothing can keep me down!"

April 17

Yet in all these things we are more
than conquerors through Him who loved us.

Romans 8:37

I am more than a conqueror!
Jesus has already won the battle against the devil.
When Jesus died, Satan couldn't hold Him down!
He rose again!
He went to heaven and sent His power back to me!
So Satan can't hold me down, either!
I will keep on believing God.
I will keep on trusting in His Word.
In Jesus' name I walk in VICTORY!

April 18
Let each of you look out not only for his own interests, but also for the interests of others.

Philippians 2:4

I am not in this world just for myself.
Others around need my love. Others need my smiles.
Sometimes they need a hug or a pat on the back.
I will look around and see where I can be a blessing.
I can make a difference in someone's life every day!

April 19
You ask and do not receive, because you ask amiss, that you may spend it on your pleasures.

James 4:3

Lord, when I pray
Your Spirit shows me what to ask for.
I am not selfish by praying only for things I want.
My prayers are for the lives and needs of others, too.
I know that when I'm thinking of You first,
and remembering others with love,
You will give me all the things I really need.
I will receive, because I want what You want!

April 20

For our citizenship is in heaven...

Philippians 3:20

My Father God has prepared a home for me in heaven.
It's more gorgeous than the biggest mansion on earth!
I live in the earth now, but I'm a CITIZEN of heaven!
I will do all I can to glorify God while I'm here.
But no matter where I am or what I'm doing,
I'll remember that my real home is waiting
for me in heaven!

April 21

Let the saints be joyful in glory!

Psalm 149:5

When I get to heaven,
I'm going to meet all of God's heroes!
I'm going to be friends with Abraham and Sarah,
Noah, Samuel, Ruth and David...John, Peter and Paul!
If Brother Enoch comes up and asks me,
"Did you read about me in the Bible?"
I'll say, "Yes, Sir!"
If Queen Esther asks, "Did you read about me?"
I'll say, "Yes, Ma'am!"
It will be wonderful!
Everyone will know me,
and I'll know them too!

April 22

Therefore, if anyone is in Christ, he is a new creation;
old things have passed away; behold,
all things have become new.

2 Corinthians 5:17

I am a spiritual being.
I live in a body, but the real ME is my spirit!
When I received Jesus, my spirit was born again.
I became part of God and He became part of me.
The power of God's Spirit is in my spirit!
The love of God is in my spirit!
My spirit can control the way I think, speak and act.
I will let God's power rule my spirit, my soul and my body!

April 23

You shall love the Lord your God with all your heart,
with all your soul, and with all your might.

Deuteronomy 6:5

I am a spirit. The life of God is in my spirit.
My spirit will live forever!
I have a soul. My soul is my mind and my thoughts.
I live in a body. My body is a house for my spirit
and my soul. I will take good care of my body
because God's Spirit lives in it like a temple.
I will protect my mind, because the way I think and believe
makes me different from those
who are not Christians.
I will guard my spirit by letting Jesus
be Lord of all my life!

April 24
Beloved, I pray that you may prosper
in all things and be in health,
just as your soul prospers.

3 John 2

When I received Jesus, my spirit was made brand new,
but my soul was not. I have to train my soul!
I must feed it with the Word of God.
I must exercise it with faith, prayer and worship.
I must guard my thoughts and keep them pure.
I will make decisions which honor Jesus.
Every day my soul will prosper and grow stronger!

April 25

For you were bought at a price; therefore glorify
God in your body and in your spirit, which are God's.

1 Corinthians 6:20

Jesus bought me.
He paid for my life with His own blood.
My spirit, my soul and my body belong to God.
I will keep my body pure.
No cigarettes or alcohol or
drugs will get into my body.
I will stay away from
places that would harm my body.
I will glorify God
in what I say, and what I do, and where I go!
I belong to JESUS!

April 26

Not lagging in diligence, fervent in spirit, serving the Lord...

Romans 12:11

I'm a worker for the Lord! I'm not lazy!
I am diligent at home, at school, everywhere!
I'm in training for an important job from the Lord!
I am full of energy for Jesus! I am faithful!
Jesus can count on me when He needs me!
I'm ready, willing and able to help change the world!

April 27

Distributing to the needs of the saints...

Romans 12:13

Saints are people who are doing God's work.
They need money just like we need money in my family.
They have places to go, people in need to help and bills to pay.
I want to help the workers who spread the gospel!
Whenever I get money, I will give some away to the saints.
I will help cover the world with God's good news!

April 28

I will bless the Lord who has given me counsel; my heart also instructs me in the night seasons.

Psalm 16:7

Bless You, Lord!
Your Word always tells me the right thing to do.
I always look to You first for advice.
You speak to my spirit and I know Your voice!
Even when I am asleep I hear from You.
I grow in wisdom daily as Your Word grows in me.
I make good choices because Your Holy Spirit guides me!

April 29

For God has not given us a spirit of fear, but of power and of love and of a sound mind.

2 Timothy 1:7

God has given me POWER!
I have authority over the devil, in Jesus' name!
God has given me His LOVE. I have no fear of anything.
God's presence surrounds me like a wall of protection.
God has given me a SOUND MIND.
I am free from confusion, guilt or worry.
I am full of faith and confidence!
Glory to God forever!

April 30

*...rather to be absent from the body
and to be present with the Lord.*

2 Corinthians 5:8

I am a spirit. I live my life on earth in this body.
When I die, my spirit will leave my earthly body.
My spirit—the REAL ME—will go instantly to Jesus!
The real me will live forever!
The real me will never die!
When all the Christians on earth go to heaven,
Jesus will give us brand new bodies.
Our new bodies will be much better than our old ones!
We'll all be happy, healthy and strong forever!

May 1

And do not be conformed to
this world, but be transformed
by the renewing of your mind, that
you may prove what is that good and
acceptable and perfect will of God.

Romans 12:2

The Lord of creation lives in me!
My mind is renewed daily by His living Word!
I'm learning to think like Jesus thinks!
I don't have to live like the world tells people to live.
I have a better way! I'll show the world
how people who love Jesus live!
I'll prove that the best road to follow is found
on God's ROAD MAP—THE BIBLE!

May 2

Therefore God also has highly exalted Him and
given Him the name which is above every name.

Philippians 2:11

Jesus! Jesus! Jesus! Oh, how I love Jesus!
Angels worship Him. Saints adore Him.
Demons tremble before His name.
The Maker of heaven and earth is my Savior!
My mouth is full of His praises.
My lips sing and shout for joy!
My knees bow in worship.
For great is my wonderful Lord!

May 3   123

Now to Him who is able to do exceedingly
abundantly above all that we ask or think,
according to the power that works in us...

Ephesians 3:20

God can do great things through me! Whenever I say
"YES!" to Him, I open the door so His power can work!
He can use me more than I ever thought possible.
He can use my faith to move mountains.
I can pray for the sick, and bring hope to the lost.
God is able to use me because I have a willing heart
and an obedient life!

May 4   124

Bless the Lord, you His angels, who excel in strength
who do His Word, heeding the voice of His Word.

Psalm 103:20

God has given me His Word to help me grow strong.
God is always listening to hear if I speak His Word.
He has told the angels to be listening for His Word, too.
As I SPEAK THE WORD OF GOD, the angels get busy!
They help bring about what I'm saying in faith.
Thank You, Lord, for all the ways
You help me to live in victory!

May 5

"I chose you and appointed you that you should go and bear fruit, and that your fruit should remain, that whatever you ask the Father in My name He may give you."

125

John 15:16

Jesus, it's AWESOME that YOU CHOSE ME!
I will do my best to live up to Your faith in me!
I'll go and bear fruit in Your name.
The fruit You help me produce is good fruit.
It will remain. The things I do to bring honor
to You will last long after the things of the world
are gone! Thank You, Jesus, for trusting me!

May 6

Be of the same mind toward one another.

126

Romans 12:16

Through the blood of Jesus, I am a brother/sister
to all Christians in God's family.
God sees me just the same as He sees everyone else.
He loves us all the same.
He corrects and teaches each of us.
None of us is better or higher up than another.
I will look at every person through God's eyes.
Every single person is valuable and precious!

May 7

Ask of Me, and I will give you the nations
for your inheritance.

Psalm 2:8

I love the people of this world!
I want to be a part of what God is doing.
I spread God's love. I pray for all the people
who don't know Jesus. I ask for souls to be saved!
I claim my neighbors! I claim friends and teachers!
I'm going to be involved in world-shaking revival!
God said to ask for souls and I would receive!
When I get to heaven, I'll look around and see
PEOPLE who are there BECAUSE I HELPED!

May 8

Only let your conduct be worthy of the gospel
of Christ... stand fast in one spirit, with one mind
striving together for the faith of the gospel.

Philippians 1:27

My behavior represents the gospel of Jesus.
For some people, the only Jesus they can imagine
is the Jesus they see in my actions.
I have a big responsibility! My words will be kind.
The way I treat others will show God's goodness.
The light of Jesus will shine through me!

May 9

If a man vows a vow to the Lord, or swears an oath to bind himself by some agreement, he shall not break his word; he shall do according to all that proceeds out of his mouth.

Numbers 30:2

When I make a promise, I keep my word.
God looks at promises very seriously. He always
keeps His promises! He never changes His mind.
So when I say I'll do something, I do it!
God's Spirit will remind me to keep my word.
God and others will know they can trust me!

May 10

That we should no longer be children, tossed to and fro...but speaking the truth in love, may grow up in all things into Him who is the head—Christ...

Ephesians 4:14a,15

I am growing up in the things of God.
I speak the truth! Lies have no place in me!
The devil might tempt me, but he can't make me lie!
I have control! The choice is mine!
I choose the way of truth!
I will always be blessed by my truthfulness,
because people will know they can believe what I say!

May 11

Trust in the Lord, and do good; dwell in the land,
and feed on His faithfulness. Delight yourself also in
the Lord, and He shall give you the desires of your heart.

Psalm 37:3,4

Lord Jesus, I trust in You. I do good.
I meditate on Your Word. I think about You all day.
I delight myself in knowing You as my Friend!
You shall direct all my steps.
Serving You will give me a happy, fruitful life.
You know all the desires of my heart, and You will give
them to me in Your timing. Thank You, Jesus.

May 12

But the prayer of the upright is His delight.

Proverbs 15:8b

God loves to hear me pray!
He's happy when I talk to Him about just anything.
He is pleased when I pray about the needs of others.
I can talk to God anytime, day or night.
He is always listening.
God answers my prayers because I am His child!

May 13

1 Peter 3:10-12 (Personalized)

I will see God's goodness all the days of my life!
I will keep my tongue from evil;
my lips will speak no lies.
I will not follow evil but will do good.
I will seek peace and pursue it.
For the eyes of the Lord are upon me;
His ears are open to my prayers.
He will deliver me from every trouble!

May 14

A merry heart does good, like medicine,
but a broken spirit dries the bones.

Proverbs 17:22

I am full of the joy of the Lord!
I have a merry heart!
I'm so happy that sadness can't come in!
Sickness runs away from me!
Trusting the Lord turns worries into joys!
Joy in my heart is like good medicine to my body!
The joy of the Lord is my strength!

May 15

"See, I have set the land before you; go in and possess the land which the Lord swore to your fathers to give to them and their descendants after them."

Deuteronomy 1:8

God plans for me to have an abundant life! A good home,
an education, health, safety and a long life are mine!
But the devil doesn't want me to receive anything!
I must use God's weapons and drive off the devil!
I'll wear God's armor! I'll pray with power!
I'll use the sword of the Spirit on the devil!
That robber can't hold my blessings back!
I will receive all God intends for me to have in Jesus' name!

May 16

For we dare not class ourselves or compare ourselves with those who commend themselves. They...are not wise.

2 Corinthians 10:12

I don't compare myself with other people.
God has given ME special gifts and talents.
He has given OTHERS special gifts and talents.
All of our abilities come FROM HIM.
I'll compare myself with what GOD expects of me.
I will work hard to do all I'm able to do
with the abilities God gave me!
That's the way I will be successful!

May 17

That the genuineness of your faith,
being much more precious than gold
that perishes, though it is tested by fire,
may be found to praise, honor, and glory at
the revelation of Jesus Christ.

1 Peter 1:17

My faith is more precious than gold!
My faith assures me that I belong to Jesus!
My faith convinces me that God's promises will happen
if I don't doubt. God will test my faith.
He tests me because He wants me to grow STRONG in faith
I will be valuable in God's kingdom,
because my faith is always growing stronger!

May 18

Oh, how I love Your law!
It is my meditation all the day.

Psalm 119:97

Lord, Your Word plants Your wisdom in me.
Knowing Your Word gives me godly understanding.
Hearing Your Word increases my faith.
Your Word lightens my path and shows me which way to go.
In Your Word are the answers to all of my concerns.
Thank You, Lord, for giving me Your Word—the Bible.

May 19

"And when you offer a sacrifice of thanksgiving to the Lord, offer it of your own free will."

Leviticus 22:29

I love to give to God! When I put money into the church, I'm showing the Lord that I am thankful. I'm saying that I appreciate all the wonderful things He has given me! My giving back to God will help get the things done that He wants to do in the earth. Every bit that I give will be helping someone, somewhere to know Jesus.

May 20

Looking for the blessed hope and glorious appearing of our great God and Savior Jesus Christ, who gave Himself for us, that He might redeem us from every lawless deed and purify for Himself His own people, zealous for good works.

Titus 2:13,14

I belong to Jesus! He gave His own life to rescue ME from the devil! I love Jesus with all my heart! I'm excited about serving the Lord! He's my HERO! When I see Jesus, I'm going to give Him ten thousand hugs and kisses! I'll worship and praise Him and dance for joy! I love You, Jesus! I love You! I love You! I love You!

May 21

"However, when He, the Spirit of truth,
has come He will guide you into all truth...

John 16:13

Holy Spirit, You are my helper. I trust You.
You will guide me into all truth.
I will not be deceived by the lies of the devil.
I hear Your voice in my spirit.
I'm growing sensitive in knowing Your voice,
because I test all my thoughts by God's Word.
As I listen and obey I will be mighty in the Lord!

May 22

And this I pray, that your love may abound still
more and more in knowledge and all discernment...

Philippians 1:9

Thank You, Holy Spirit, for spiritual discernment.
You help me to know in my heart what is right and wrong.
I am able to tell which people are Christ-like
and which ones are only pretending.
I know who are my real friends and who are not.
I recognize the plans of the devil and I resist them.
I love the things of God, and I walk in His truth!

May 23

Therefore, my beloved brethren, let every man be swift to hear, slow to speak, slow to wrath; for the wrath of man does not produce the righteousness of God.

143

James 1:19,20

In order to please God, I need to act like Jesus!
I'm not fussy or angry! I'm patient and peaceful!
I'm learning when to talk and when to stay quiet.
I am a good listener! I am polite.
I don't say foolish things.
My words are uplifting and encouraging.
I am swift to hear, slow to get angry
and quick to walk in love!

May 24

Let no corrupt communication proceed out of your mouth, but what is good for necessary edification, that it may impart grace to the hearers.

144

Ephesians 4:29

I bless others with the words of my mouth!
I let them know they are important. I tell them when they do a nice job! I am sincere and truthful.
The words I say come from my heart.
I find something good to say about everyone.
Those who hear me will be encouraged!

May 25

145

Guard what was committed to your trust, avoiding the profane and vain babblings and contradictions of what is falsely called knowledge...

1 Timothy 6:20

I will guard the treasures God has given me!
He has given me salvation: I'll walk close to Jesus!
He has given me health: I will take care of my body!
He has given me His Holy Spirit:
I will use my authority against works of darkness!
He has given me the Bible: I will use my knowledge
of His Word to live a holy, fruitful life!

May 26

146

And let us not grow weary while doing good, for in due season we shall reap if we do not lose heart.

Galatians 6:9

I will never get tired of serving God! People may not
understand me. Some will say I'm different. They may
even make fun of me. Well, I AM different!
I don't belong to this world! I belong to God!
When people around me have a problem,
when they are afraid or lonely, they will come to me.
They know I have the answer they need: JESUS.

May 27

As you have therefore received Christ Jesus
the Lord, so walk in Him, rooted and built up
in Him and established in the faith...

Colossians 2:6,7a

I walk in the knowledge of Christ Jesus, my Lord!
I am like a tree with STRONG ROOTS. My roots are
in Jesus, so I will grow, GROW, G-R-O-W!
I will produce good works that glorify God.
My life will make a difference on the earth!

May 28

What then shall we say to these things?
If God is for us, who can be against us?

Romans 8:31

Lots of things go on in the world that are not good.
Both the newspaper and the Bible tell of the world's evils.
The Bible also says God is FOR me! He is on my side!
No plans of the devil can defeat me!
I look to the Lord first in all I do.
I am strong in the power of His might!
If God is FOR me, WHO can be against me?!!

May 29

A good name is to be chosen rather than great riches.

Proverbs 22:1

God knew my name before I was ever born!
Jesus has my name written in His book in heaven!
My family, friends and teachers all know me by name.
I will live in such a way that people will think
good thoughts when they hear my name!
They will remember me for the kind things I do.
When others think of me, they'll be happy to know me!

May 30

Rejoice in the Lord always. Again I will say, rejoice!

Philippians 4:4

I just love the Lord to pieces!
Words can't even tell how much Jesus means to me!
I praise Him all day long! I can't stop singing!
Jesus peps me up! He makes me feel good!
He likes me for who I am! His arms are always open!
He loves me, He wants me, He corrects me, He forgives me!
There is no one else like Jesus!

June 7

Give, and it will be given to you...With the same measure that you use, it will be measured back to you.

Luke 6:38

I am a GIVER! I'm not selfish. No way!
I have a thankful heart, so I love to give!
I know God is happy when I give my blessings away,
because He keeps giving me more to give!
God and I both keep giving and giving!
I'm letting God use ME to spread His love around!

June 8

And if anyone does not obey our word in this epistle, note that person and do not keep company with him.

2 Thessalonians 3:14

I notice people who obey God.
I also notice those who don't obey Him.
I model my life after the wise people who serve God.
I don't keep company with those who are foolish.
I correct them in love. I pray for them.
But I spend my time with people
who let Jesus rule their life.

June 9

Have mercy upon me, O God,
according to Your lovingkindness; according to
the multitude of Your tender mercies.
Blot out my transgressions.

Psalm 51:1

Lord, I know when I do wrong things.
Sometimes I try to hide them. But You always know!
The only way I can be happy again is to let
You know I'm really sorry for what I've done.
You always accept me! You always forgive me!
You clean me up and point me in the right direction!
I really try not to sin. But if ever I do,
I will always run TO You, and never away FROM You!

June 10

For whom the Lord loves He corrects, just
as a father the son in whom he delights.

Proverbs 3:12

Father God, I submit myself to You.
I want to do what is pleasing to You.
If I do something wrong, I want You to correct me.
You know what is best for me.
I will always give You power over my life,
because I trust You. Amen!

June 11

"As the Father loved me, I also have loved you, abide in My love...that your joy may be full."

John 15:9-11

Jesus is my leader! I do what He tells me!
I walk in love toward everyone.
I show them how much God cares about them.
The more love I give away, the more joy I have!
Giving love always brings good results!
Love never fails!

June 12

I will both lie down in peace, and sleep;
for You alone, O Lord, make me dwell in safety.

Psalm 4:8

Thank You, Lord, for watching over me while I sleep.
I never feel alone! You are with me all the time.
My BIG, BIG angel is right in my room with me, too!
I'm not afraid of the dark. I'm not worried about dreams.
My dreams will be peaceful, bright and happy!
Only good thoughts will come into my mind!
Good night, Lord!

June 13

...from whom the whole body,
joined and knit together by what every joint
supplies, according to the effective working by
which every part does its share...

Ephesians 4:16

I am a part of the body of Christ.
The body of Christ means all of us Christians!
Jesus is the head! He tells the body what to do!
I have a special job to do to help the Body grow strong.
I'm the only one who can do my job in my own special way.
God needs me. The body of Christ needs me!
I will do my share. Jesus can depend on me!

June 14

...and every gifted artisan in whom the Lord has
put wisdom and understanding, to know how to do
all manner of work for the service of the sanctuary...

Exodus 36:1

When God asks me to do something,
He will give me the ability to do it!
As I grow and try to please God, He will
show me HOW and WHEN and WHAT to do for Him.
I'm ABLE to succeed, because God's ability is in me!

June 15

"If you can believe, all things are possible to him who believes."

Mark 9:23

Jesus, I BELIEVE You died to give me eternal life.
I BELIEVE You were beaten so I could be healed.
I BELIEVE the power of Your Holy Spirit is in me.
Everything I need, I BELIEVE You will provide.
Power, faith, miracles: All are easy for You!
With God, nothing is impossible!

June 16

Surely He has borne our griefs and carried our sorrows...and by His stripes we are healed.

Isaiah 53:4,5

I resist the spirit of infirmity in the name of Jesus!
Devil, you can't put sickness on me! I'm God's property!
God doesn't give sickness; He gives healing.
Jesus was beaten with a whip for my sicknesses.
The Bible says BY HIS STRIPES I AM HEALED.
Thank You, Jesus, for what You did for me.
Thank You for a strong, healthy body!

June 17

Therefore we also, since we are surrounded by so great a cloud of witnesses...let us run with endurance the race that is set before us.

Hebrews 12:1

I have relatives who have already gone to heaven.
They know whenever I do something that pleases God!
God lets them see whenever my life glorifies Him.
My great-great-grandparents are up there cheering
for me! They are praying for me, too!
They want me to be a winner for God!

June 18

...the Lord Jesus Christ who will transform our lowly body that it may be conformed to His glorious body...

Philippians 3:21

When I get to heaven I'll have a new body just like Jesus has!
My new body will never get a runny nose!
No more tummy aches! No measles or chickenpox! My new body
won't even get scratches if I fall out of a heavenly tree!
I will always be young, strong and healthy!
I will never die! Hallelujah!

June 19

The eyes of all look expectantly to You, and You give them their food in due season. You open Your hand and satisfy the desire of every living thing.

Psalm 145:16

The Lord is full of mercy.
He hears the prayers of all who call on Him.
He has compassion upon the poor and the hungry.
He prepares food to send to their tables.
The Lord gives hope. His faithfulness is everlasting!

170

June 20

Do all things without murmuring and disputing.

Philippians 2:14

Complaining takes away joy. Yikes!
I don't want to lose my joy!
I'll try harder to be a cheerful helper!
I will clean my room and sing!
I'll do my homework with a merry heart!
I'm blessed to be ABLE to do
all the things I am asked to do.
I'll walk in an "attitude of gratitude!"

171

June 21

(God has) raised us up together,
and made us sit together in the
heavenly places in Christ Jesus.

172

Ephesians 2:6

I'm flying high with Jesus!
God has raised me up into heavenly places!
Jesus is my pilot! He's training me to be His co-pilot!
He guides me through the dark clouds,
and shows me how to break through
into the brightness of victory!
Obstacles may be in my way,
not every flight may be smooth...
But, Jesus and I will arrive right on time!

June 22

Because Your lovingkindness is better than life,
my lips shall praise You...I will lift up
my hands in Your name.

173

Psalm 68:3,4

Dear Lord, You are my God!
I remember You early in the morning.
I think about You as I go to sleep at night.
Your love for me fills my heart with music!
My lips will sing praise to Your mighty name!
I will lift up my hands and rejoice!
There is no one as wonderful as my God!

June 23

In the multitude of words sin is not lacking,
but he who restrains his lips is wise.

Proverbs 10:19

I look for good things to talk about.
I don't tell bad reports about other people.
If I can't say something nice,
I just won't say anything at all.
I am a peacemaker! I'm a giver of good news!

June 24

"Judge not, that you be not judged. For with
what judgment you judge, you will be judged.

Matthew 7:1,2a

I will not judge other people.
I don't know what is in someone else's heart.
My job is not to criticize others.
My job is to share God's love and forgiveness!
I'll be someone others can talk to,
someone they can trust.
When their heart is ready, I'll be
able to lead them to the Lord.

June 25

"Everyone who exalts himself will be abased, and he who humbles himself will be exalted."

Luke 18:14b

My righteousness comes from my Lord Jesus Christ!
Any goodness I have is from His Spirit in me.
I need God's help every day!
God gives me the desire to do His will.
Jesus is the source of all my power!
Without Him I can do nothing...
but WITH HIM I can do anything He asks!

June 26

O Lord, You have searched me and known me...
You understand my thought afar off...
You are acquainted with all my ways.

Psalm 139:1-3

Lord, You know me better than anyone else.
You search my heart. You know my inner thoughts.
You know when I'm awake or asleep.
You understand all of my concerns.
You are aware of all my hopes, needs and desires.
You're always with me, loving me, thinking about me
and caring for me. Thank You, precious Lord.
I love You.

June 27

And blessed is he who is not offended because of Me.

Luke 7:23

I am proud to be a Christian!
My life is a joy because I know Jesus!
How could I deny Jesus when He's my best Friend?
I'll ALWAYS look for ways to tell others about Him!
I want the whole world to know
the most important Person in my life!

June 28

He who made me in the womb,
Does he not see my ways, and count all my steps?

Job 31:4,15

The God of creation made me. He gave me life inside my
mother. He sees all my ways. He counts all my steps.
If I step out of His path, He warns me.
If I were in the darkest forest, He would see me.
If I were lost in a crowd of strangers,
God would know, and He would take care of me.
I put my trust totally in God.
No matter what situation I am in,
I KNOW my heavenly Father will rescue me!

June 29

Bless the Lord, O my soul,
and forget not all His benefits.

Psalm 103:2

I will bless You, O Lord!
When I think of You, my spirit leaps for joy!
I could never forget all You have done for me.
You rescued me from the devil! You forgave all my sins.
You heal me whenever I get sick. You keep me from harm.
You crown me with Your lovingkindness.
Thank You, Lord! I'll rejoice in You forever!

June 30

Romans 8:37-39 (Personalized)

In all things I am more than a conqueror
through Jesus who loves me!
For I am convinced that neither death nor life,
nor angels nor principalities nor powers,
nor things present nor things to come,
nor height nor depth,
nor any other created thing,
shall be able to separate me from the love of God
which is in Christ Jesus my Lord!

Note to Parents: A portion of the curse within the old law declared that the sins of the fathers would be visited upon their children even to several generations (see Exodus 34:7). Many Bible scholars agree that this does not mean God punishes children for the sins of their parents, but that if unprotected, the child may be open to demonic activities which had controlled parents, grandparents or other ancestors. The protection God provides is, of course, the blood of Jesus.

The following confession is lengthy but powerful. If there is any question of controlling problems or sins in the child's ancestry, I recommend that this confession be spoken over and spoken by the child. And because we know Satan will often leave for a season and then try to return, periodic faith-filled declarations of these words can certainly do no harm.

July 1

Christ has redeemed us from the curse of the law,
having become a curse for us...that the blessing of Abraham
might come upon the Gentiles in Christ Jesus, that
we might receive the promise of the Spirit through faith.

Galatians 3:13a,14

Father, Your Word says that when I accepted Jesus I was
redeemed from the curse of the law. Part of the old law said
that sins of the parents would come upon the children for
many generations.

I don't know all my ancestors. I don't know if they did bad or
good deeds in their lives. I want to be sure I have no curse from
the devil on my life, because of anything someone else in my family has done.

So, in the name of Jesus of Nazareth,
I break any power of the devil over my life!
I break the power of any sin from any past generations.
I resist any curse the devil has tried to put on
our family!

I am free in Jesus!
I'm a new creation!
I am washed in the blood of the Lord Jesus Christ.
No evil can hinder my life.
I have authority over the devil.
He has no authority over me!
Jesus, You are my Lord!
You live in me, and I live in You!
I am redeemed!
Thank You, Jesus!

The Lord is my shepherd; I shall not want.

Psalm 23

The Lord is my Shepherd.
I am His little sheep.
He takes care of me.
He sees all I need, and He provides for me.
He encourages me when I feel upset.
He fills me with His peace.
He guides my steps,
so I don't get tricked by the evil one.
No matter what happens in the world around me
I have no fear. For my Lord is with me.
He comforts me with His presence.
He anoints my life with
the power of His Holy Spirit.
He pours blessings all over me!
The goodness of the Lord
will go with me all the days of my life.
Then I will live in the house of the Lord forever.

July 3

Behold, the eye of the Lord is on those who
fear Him, on those who hope in His mercy.

Psalm 33:18

The eyes of the Lord are on me, because I love Him!
He watches over me because I trust in His mercy.
He keeps me from harm. He provides all I need to live.
The Lord is my help and my shield.
My heart rejoices in trusting Him!
I will bless His holy name forever!

July 4

We know that whoever is born of God does not sin;
but he who has been born of God keeps himself,
and the wicked one does not touch him.

1 John 5:18

The devil can't touch me!
Because of Jesus, I am born of God.
I am GOD'S PROPERTY!
No plans of the devil can overtake me,
God leads me! His Spirit warns me! Angels protect me!
Thank You, Jesus, for Your power in me!
I have everything I need to overcome the devil!

July 5

Let love be without hypocrisy.
Abhor what is evil. Cling to what is good.

Romans 12:9

I will never pretend to love someone just to get my way.
I won't be nice in order to receive something in return.
I give love and kindness without expecting anything back.
I do it just so I can be like Jesus.
Jesus is good and merciful because He really loves us.
I will model my actions after Jesus.

July 6

Do not be unequally yoked together with
unbelievers. "Come out from among them
and be separate, says the Lord."

2 Corinthians 6:14,17a

I am a witness to unbelievers. I love and pray for them.
But Jesus said for me to be separate from the world.
I won't let myself talk or act like unbelievers.
I must keep my life pure and clean to represent Jesus.
I will choose friends who love Jesus. I will grow up
and marry someone who is a joyful, strong Christian!
We'll have a God-centered life and family in Jesus' name!

July 7

...forgetting those things which are behind and reaching forward to those things which are ahead, I press toward the goal for the prize of the upward call of God in Christ Jesus.

Philippians 3:13,14

Jesus, You are the healer of all bad things. You come to those who need You. You make them new again. You give hope and direction for the future. Thank You for taking away the hurt from any bad things that have ever happened to me. I will not remember the bad, only the good. I put my hand in Your hand, Lord. I will be full of Your hope and joy, as we go through life together. Amen.

July 8

How precious also are your thoughts to me, O God!

Psalm 139:17

How precious You are to me, dear Lord.
I think about You all the time.
I remember how You died for my sins.
I think of the pain You felt, and the blood You shed.
I imagine what it would have been like to sit on
Your lap, with You telling Your wonderful stories.
Everything You did was just to let people
know how much God really loves them.
Thank You, Jesus. I love You.

July 9

For to me, to live is Christ.

Philippians 1:21

Lord Jesus,
You are the reason I was born.
My heavenly Father wanted me to be alive
so I could accept You and become His child!
He wanted to pour His love on me and give
me an important purpose in His kingdom.
I have joy and hope and excitement about the future!

July 10

Then Paul answered, "...I am ready not only
to be bound but also to die at Jerusalem
for the name of the Lord Jesus."

Acts 21:13

Dear Lord, Your disciple Paul loved You so much, he was
willing even to die for Your name. He wouldn't deny You.
He would not stop preaching. Help me, Jesus,
to be true to You. Even if people make fun of me for being a Christian,
I will still tell them You love them. I would rather have a few friends
who serve You than a hundred friends who serve
the devil! Help me to be a good example to others.
Thank You for the boldness and courage to always live for You!

July 11

Children, obey your parents in all things,
for this is well pleasing to the Lord.

Colossians 3:20

When I obey my parents,
that's one way of obeying God!
I make God happy when I listen to my parents.
He is proud of me and blesses me.
Obeying my parents is one way I can say,
"I LOVE YOU!" to them and "I LOVE YOU!" to God!

July 12

For out of the abundance of the heart his mouth speaks.

Luke 6:45b

Whatever goes through my eyes or ears goes into my heart.
I have a watchguard on my heart! I read only nice books.
I watch only wholesome programs on TV or videos.
I listen to happy, healthy music.
God's Spirit helps me to know
which things are good for me and which are not.
I do not allow evil to get into my spirit.
My heart is full of good treasures!

July 13

Great peace have those who love Your
law, and nothing causes them to stumble.

Psalm 119:165

I rejoice in God's Word, as one who has found a great
treasure. I love God's Word because God tells the truth!
I have great peace, because God's Word is in me.
Even if I make mistakes, God helps me out.
He never laughs at me. He's always there to lift me up.
Nothing can cause me to fail in life,
because I put God first!

July 14

Moreover the law entered that the offense
might abound. But where sin abounded,
grace abounded much more.

Romans 5:20

Thank You, Lord that I have a free will.
I want to make the right choices, but sometimes I don't.
When I make wrong decisions, You are still with me.
Your Spirit hugs me and loves me and forgives me.
I always feel Your comfort and Your peace when
I say, "I'm sorry, Lord." You always make things OK again.

July 15

He who has pity on the poor lends to the Lord,
and He will pay back what he has given.

Proverbs 19:17

I am so-o-o blessed!
I have more than I need of everything!
I feel sad when I think of children who don't have enough
clothes to wear, or food to eat, or toys to play with.
I will share from all I have. I'll be a giver of blessings.
The Lord will bless me back, and then I'll give some more!

July 16

For the wages of sin is death, but the gift of God
is eternal life in Christ Jesus our Lord.

Romans 6:28

Lord, in Jesus' name I pray for those who don't know You.
Send Your workers everywhere to help people get born again.
Help me to be one of Your workers!
I don't want anyone to be lost.
Help me to show others Jesus is the way to eternal life.
Give me opportunities to witness, and boldness to speak!
Thank You, Jesus. I'll be working together with You!

July 17

But let patience have its perfect work, that you may be perfect and complete, lacking nothing...Every good gift and every perfect gift is from above, and comes down from the Father.

James 1:4,17

I am growing in patience!
I pray every day, for myself and for others.
Sometimes my prayers are answered right away,
and sometimes I have to wait.
If I have to wait, my faith stays strong.
I know God is working on everything I've asked
if it is based on His Word. By faith I receive
all the good and perfect gifts my Father has for me!

July 18

But you, beloved, building yourselves up on your most holy faith, praying in the Holy Spirit...

Jude 20

My faith is holy to God.
God is pleased when I use my faith and trust Him.
ONE way I grow strong in faith is by hearing God's Word.
Putting His Word in my heart gives me spiritual muscles!
ANOTHER way I grow strong in faith is by praying.
The more I pray in the Holy Spirit, the stronger I get.
The stronger I get, the more God can use me!

July 19

"Assuredly, I say to you, inasmuch as you did it to one of the least of these My brethren, you did it to Me."

Matthew 25:35,40

When I give food to the hungry, I am feeding Jesus.
When I give clothes to the poor, I'm clothing Jesus.
When I give offerings so the lost can hear
God's Word, I am giving to Jesus.
Jesus loves every person so much, that whenever I bless
someone else, Jesus says I am blessing Him.
I AM SHOWING JESUS I LOVE HIM BY
THE LOVE I SHOW TO OTHERS.

July 20

Blessed be the Lord, because He has heard the voice of my supplications.

Psalm 28:6

Lord, I bless Your name!
You hear all my cries. You see all my tears.
You know all my needs, large and small.
My heart trusts in You, and You always help me.
Therefore, my heart greatly rejoices!
With my hands lifted up and with songs of joy
I will praise You!

July 21

"Take heed that you do not do your
charitable deeds before men,
to be seen by them."

Matthew 6:1,5

Lord, when I do good things, it's NOT so people will see me.
I'll set a good example, so people can see YOU, not ME.
When I give my offerings, it's because I want to serve You.
The prayers I pray come from the love in my heart.
I don't care about impressing people!
I want to do all I can to please You, because I love You.

July 22

"Do not be afraid; only believe."

Mark 5:36b

God has all power in heaven and earth!
He is always ready to use His power for me!
No matter what happens, I will trust God.
I believe in God's ability to work everything out.
All that concerns me is in His hands!

July 23

"Be angry, and do not sin:" do not let the sun go down on your wrath, nor give place to the devil.

Ephesians 4:26,27

If someone makes me angry, I do not stay mad.
I forgive as quick as a wink! I don't stay upset!
Hurt and anger take away my joy, my peace and my strength.
I won't let the devil get that kind of hold on me!
When I keep loving and forgiving, the devil scrams!
God's peace rushes in! I'm a QUICK FORGIVER!

July 24

"Whoever desires to become great among you, let him be your servant."

Matthew 20:26

If I want to be great in God's kingdom, I'll first be a
servant. I will be loving even when others are unkind.
I'll be obedient when it would be easier to disobey.
I'll be dependable and not lazy. I'll use time wisely.
I am willing to give my time, my love, my life
to help God accomplish His will on the earth.
This is the way my life will have purpose and success.

July 25
Whoever has no rule over
his own spirit is like a city
broken down, without walls.

Proverbs 25:28

My spirit is like a city with STRONG WALLS!
I guard what enters my spirit through my eyes and
ears so no evil can break down the walls of protection.
NO ENEMIES can come in to destroy God's work in me!
Good or evil can enter me through my five senses...so,
I'm making sure to let the good IN and keep the evil OUT!

July 26

Beloved, do not believe every spirit, but test
the spirits, whether they are of God...

1 John 4:1

Jesus teaches me to test all I hear and see.
He helps me to know truth from lies. The devil is a liar.
Some people serve the devil, so they tell lies.
All things I SEE on TV or books are not always the truth.
All things that I HEAR may not be true.
I will listen to God's Word in my heart.
I'll depend on His Word to guide me.
God will keep me from being deceived.

July 27

Then we who are alive and remain shall be caught up together with them in the clouds to meet the Lord in the air. And thus we shall always be with the Lord.

1 Thessalonians 4:17

I will always be with the Lord!
He is WITH ME while I live on earth.
And I'll be WITH HIM when I go to heaven!
If Jesus returns to earth in my lifetime,
I'll go right up into the sky to meet Him!
He will take me and all Christians instantly to heaven!

July 28

For if we believe that Jesus died and rose again, even so God will bring with Him those who sleep in Jesus.

1 Thessalonians 4:14

If Jesus waits a long time to return to earth,
and if I die like others who have grown old and died,
I will just jump out of my body like I am taking off a
coat! The angels will take me straight to heaven.
The only people who can get to heaven are Christians.
The angels will take them when they die,
or Jesus will take them when He returns.
Either way, I'm God's child, and there's
a home in heaven especially for me!

July 29

For the word of God is living and powerful, and sharper than any two edged sword...

Hebrews 4:12

The Word of God is powerful!
It is the mighty sword I use against the devil.
The Word of God is the answer to any problem I'll ever have!
All of God's wisdom is in His Word.
He put it into the Bible so it could get into ME.
God's Word will produce mighty results in my life!
I believe it, I speak it, I act upon it in Jesus' name!

July 30

And now, little children, abide in Him, that when He appears we may have confidence and not be ashamed before Him at His coming.

1 John 2:28

Jesus is coming back soon! I'll be doing His will when He comes. I'll be praying for the lost and telling them of God's love. I'll be showing God's kindness. I'll be walking in His power and using the name of Jesus to set people free from the evil one. The harvest is ready! I have a lot of work to do! When Jesus comes, I'll be able to say, "Yes, Lord, I did what You needed me to do!"

210

211

July 31

For the weapons of our warfare are not carnal but mighty in God for pulling down strongholds.

2 Corinthians 10:4,5

The earth is a battleground!
The devil keeps trying to win.
I am God's soldier!
I will do my part!
I have mighty weapons.
The power of the Holy Spirit is in me.
God's armor covers me.
My mind is renewed by the Word of God.
I have power in my prayers.
I have authority over the devil
in the mighty name of Jesus!
God is the WINNER,
and I'm on God's side!

August 1

If then you were raised with Christ,
seek those things which are above,
where Christ is, sitting at the right hand
of God. Set your mind on things above, not on
things on the earth.

Colossians 3:1,2

Since my real home is in heaven,
I set my desires on heavenly things.
Nothing on earth is going with me to heaven!
Heaven has a lot of exciting things to keep me busy!
The only things I can take with me are human souls.
The best rewards I will have in heaven are the people
who are there with me because I told them about Jesus!

August 2

And the peace of God, which surpasses
all understanding, will guard your hearts
and minds through Christ Jesus.

Philippians 4:7

God's peace is my peace! I have no cares!
God already knows about everything that matters to me.
My trust is already in Him. So everything will be fine!
Nothing that the world offers can give me real peace.
But Jesus gives me comfort way down deep inside.
Only the Lord can make me feel so good!

August 3   215
But he who is of a merry heart has a continual feast.

Proverbs 15:15b

I am a cheer-er-upper!
When Mother gets tired, I say, "I love you, Mom!"
If Dad gets cross, I understand. I give him the hug he
needs. I'm going to look for people I can cheer up!
No matter who I run into, my smile
can make someone's day brighter!

August 4   216
"The harvest truly is plentiful, but the laborers
are few. Therefore pray the Lord of the harvest
to send out laborers into His harvest."

Matthew 9:37,38

Lord Jesus,
I pray for You to send workers all over the world, to tell
lost people about God's love. Supply all the money
Your workers need. Give them safe travel.
Send them out full of Your power and Your favor.
Let every person on earth have a chance to know You!
Let me be one of Your helpers, Lord. Amen.

August 5

Fight the good fight of faith, lay hold on eternal life, to which you were also called and have confessed the good confession in the presence of many witnesses.

1 Timothy 6:12

I fight the good fight of faith! I'm no quitter!
I keep on walking in love. I keep on praying.
I keep on sharing the gospel.
Doubt isn't allowed in my heart!
The world won't take away God's plan for my life!
I will guard my words, my actions and my integrity!
I won't lose, because God made me to win!

August 6

The Lord will perfect that which concerns me.

Psalm 138:8

Father God, in the name of Jesus,
I declare that You shall direct my life!
I will hear Your voice.
I will listen to Your instructions.
I will know Your will in all matters that concern me.
Thank You, Father, that I am special to You.
You have a plan for my life that will be perfected!

August 7

Are they not all ministering spirits sent forth
to minister for those who will inherit salvation?

Hebrews 1:14

219

God has sent angels to earth to help us.
I can't see the angels, but they are everywhere!
They are BIG, and they are MIGHTY!
When I have a need, I pray to God. If I pray in Jesus'
name, and if I pray according to God's Word, the
angels get busy and help His WORD to be fulfilled!
Angels are just one of many ways God cares for me!

August 8

But we see Jesus, who was made a little lower
than the angels, for the suffering of death
crowned with glory and honor...

Hebrews 2:9

220

God has angels working all over the earth.
One of their jobs is to protect me.
They can protect me when I'm being obedient to God.
But my trust is not in angels!
MY TRUST IS IN THE LORD!
Jesus has ALL POWER in heaven and in earth!
Angels are mighty helpers for God, but
JESUS IS LORD OF ALL!

August 9

Many are the afflictions of the righteous, But the Lord delivers him out of them all.

Psalm 34:19

God promised He would always be with me.
He said He would deliver me out of every trouble.
He didn't say my life would not have any problems!
He DID say He would help me overcome them!
I AM an overcomer! God is on my side!
Every day may not have blue skies...
but no flood is going to overtake me!
God and I can't sink!

August 10

For You are my hope, O Lord God;
You are my trust from my youth.
By You I have been upheld from my birth.

Psalm 71:5,6a

In You, O Lord, I put my trust. You have watched over me
ever since I was born. Your love has never failed me!
I will grow up in the strength and knowledge of God.
My mouth will tell of Your righteousness.
When I am old and have gray hair, I will still
be proclaiming Your faithfulness and power!

August 11

Is this not the fast I have chosen:

Isaiah 58:6

223

Fasting is giving up my own wants or needs for someone else.
I can do without a meal to spend time in prayer.
I can give God's Word to those who are in darkness.
My money can help to feed the hungry.
When I give up MYSELF to help OTHERS,
the light of Jesus shines through me
and lights up the world around me!

August 12

Then you shall call, and the Lord will answer;
you shall cry, then He will say, "Here I am."

Isaiah 58:9

224

Fasting means I put God's desires first and not my own.
I look to see where I can be a blessing.
I treat every person as a valuable treasure.
I feel the love of God coming from HIS heart
and going out through MY heart to others.
This is why I'm so full of joy, and my
life has fulfillment and peace.

August 13

Therefore humble yourselves
under the mighty hand of God,
that He may exalt you in due time, casting
all your care upon Him, for He cares for you.

1 Peter 5:6,7

I humble myself unto God. I realize I NEED Him.
I need His strength to lift up my faith.
I need His presence to give me comfort and hope.
I need His power to resist temptations from the devil.
I cast all my cares upon the Lord!
He can handle anything! My God has all the answers!

August 14

But I discipline my body and
bring it into subjection...

1 Corinthians 9:27

My body does not rule me! I rule my body!
I eat foods that are healthy and good for me.
I don't overeat! I don't fill up on junk foods!
I eat good snacks that are good for me like fruit.
I exercise daily. I make my body work hard!
I get plenty of rest so I can grow.
If I take good care of my body,
it will last me for a long, long time!

August 15

Do not lie to one another.

Colossians 3:9

I follow Jesus and not the devil! The devil invents lies.
He tells people in their minds that one little lie is OK.
But I have a choice! I choose not to listen to his lies!
Truthfulness is of God—and I belong to God—
so I tell the truth! People can believe what I say!

August 16

For we are to God the fragrance of Christ among those who are being saved and among those who are perishing.

2 Corinthians 2:15

My behavior is important to everyone around me.
Some people are just starting to learn about Jesus.
The things I do show others what Jesus is like.
The way I live my life may be the cause
of someone else changing their life!
I'll do my best to let them see Jesus in me!

August 17

(Food is) to be received with thanksgiving
by those who believe and know the truth.

1 Timothy 4:3b

Thank You, Lord, for the good foods You give me to eat.
You provide all that I need and more.
Help the poor, Lord Jesus. Use people who have plenty
to feed the hungry all over the world.
I will remember the hungry, Jesus.
I will be one who helps them.

August 18

Therefore by Him let us continually offer
the sacrifice of praise to God, that is, the fruit
of our lips, giving thanks to His name.

Hebrews 13:15

I praise God all the time!
Even when I don't feel like rejoicing,
I still praise the Lord because He loves me so much!
He has given me His life, health, joy and victory!
He has already done all for me that I'll ever need!
PRAISE THE LORD!

August 19

231

But the wisdom that is from above is first pure,
then peaceable, gentle, willing to yield, full of mercy
and good fruits, without partiality and without hypocrisy.

James 3:17

I walk in God's wisdom. I keep my life pure and clean.
I walk in peace with others. I am gentle and kind.
I am willing to let others be first.
I don't criticize or talk ugly about anyone.
Because of God's wisdom working in me,
I am like a beautiful tree that produces good fruit!

August 20

232

But the Lord is faithful, who will establish you
and guard you from the evil one.

2 Thessalonians 3:3

The Lord is faithful.
He causes His power to work for me.
He guards me from the evil one.
He directs my heart and guides my steps.
Because I want to obey and serve Him, God will
make my life happy and fruitful!

August 21

"If you love Me, keep My commandments.
And I will pray the Father, and He will give you
another Helper (who) dwells with you and will be in you."

John 14:15-17

Jesus, I love You!
I SHOW You my love by keeping Your commandments.
I honor my parents. I respect my teachers.
I walk in love. I tell the truth.
I try hard to be like You in all I do.
Thank You for sending the Holy Spirit to help me.
With Him in me, I have the power to keep Your commandments!

August 22

And have no fellowship with the unfruitful works
of darkness...it is shameful even to speak of those things.

Ephesians 5:11,12

I don't talk about the evil that goes on in the world.
I talk about the good things that God does!
I say words that give people hope.
I show others the way to God's peace.
I let them know there is nothing too big for God to handle!

It is Christ who died, and furthermore is
also risen, who is even at the right hand of God,
who also makes intercession for us.

Romans 8:34

Lord Jesus,
It sure makes me feel good to know
that You are keeping an eye on me!
While You're on Your throne in heaven,
You see whenever I need a little extra help.
You talk it over with the Father.
You send the power of God forth for me!
The angels listen to Your instructions.
I will always have whatever I need when I need it.
I walk in Your protection and Your provision.
My life is one of victory!
Thank You for interceding for me, Jesus!
I appreciate You.

September 1

Yet who knows whether you have come to the kingdom for such a time as this?

Esther 4:14b

I was born just when I was supposed to be!
God needs me right now at this time in history.
He has given me talents and abilities that
I can use in His kingdom in my own special way.
I am valuable to God because no one else is just like me!
I set my heart to be God's helper in every way I can!

September 2

...speaking to one another in psalms and hymns and spiritual songs, singing and making melody in your heart to the Lord.

Ephesians 5:19

My heart is full of songs to the Lord!
I can make up psalms just like David of the Bible.
Melodies of praise come out
when I open my mouth in worship.
God made me to be an instrument of praise.
When I worship God, the devil gets scared and leaves!
I will praise the Lord my God forever!

September 3
"For in Him we live and move and have our being."

Acts 17:28

Lord Jesus, You are the most important Person in my life.
Everything that I am is all wrapped up in You.
You are interested in all that I am involved with.
You help me in every area of my life.
Living for You is what life is all about!

September 4
...even so in Christ all shall be made alive. The body
is sown in corruption, it is raised in incorruption.
It is sown a natural body, it is raised a spiritual body.

1 Corinthians 15:22,42,44

I'm going to meet all kinds of people in heaven!
I'll know them and they'll know me. My relatives and
ancestors, even people from Bible days will know me!
Everyone will have a new body like Jesus has.
We can run, jump and play and ride a heavenly horse!
But our new bodies will never get tired or hurt!
And they'll never, never die!

September 5
"Therefore I say to you,
whatever things you ask when
you pray, believe that you receive them,
and you will have them."

Lord, You said in Your Word
for me to ask You for WHATEVER I NEED.
You're always interested and You want to bless me.
Whenever I ask, I ask according to what Your Word says.
I BELIEVE in my heart and SAY with my mouth
that my prayer is answered. Then, in Your perfect time
You do it! Hallelujah!

September 6
Therefore, brethren, stand fast and hold
the traditions which you were taught,
whether by word or our epistle.

2 Thessalonians 2:15

249

I'm standing on God's Word!
My faith can't be shaken by what I see or don't see!
God pays attention when I speak His Word.
His promises were given in truth.
He ALWAYS fulfills His Word in perfect timing!
God's words in my heart and in my mouth are mighty!

September 7

"I will...open for you the windows of heaven
and pour out for you such blessing that
there will not be room enough to receive it.
And I will rebuke the devourer for your sakes."

Malachi 3:10b,11a

God is happy when I tithe! When I give part
of my money back to Him, He knows I appreciate Him.
I give to God by putting money in church to spread
the gospel. What I give helps the poor and needy.
God opens the windows of heaven to pour blessings on me!
He keeps the devil from destroying what belongs to me!
I'm glad I'm a tither!

September 8

For it is God who works in you both to
will and to do for His good pleasure.

Philippians 2:18

Lord, I'm glad You know I'm not perfect!
You love me anyway!
You promised You'd HELP me to do Your will.
You even said You'd help me WANT to do Your will!
I really do want to please You, Father.
I'm glad we're working on me together!

September 9

I have set before you life and death, blessing and cursing; therefore choose life...cling to Him, for He is your life and the length of your days.

Deuteronomy 30:19,20

God has given me a choice:
Life or death, blessing or cursing.
Living for the devil is a curse!
Serving God is life. I CHOOSE LIFE!
Sorrows come to those trapped by the devil.
Blessings come to those who obey the Lord.
I CHOOSE BLESSINGS!
I will cling to the Lord my God.
He is my life and my joy!
I will serve Him with a happy heart forever!

September 10

Where can I go from Your Spirit? Or where can I flee from Your presence? If I take the wings of the morning and dwell in the uttermost parts of the sea, even there Your hand shall lead me, and Your right hand shall hold me.

Psalm 139:7,9,10

My Lord and my God...
Where can I go that You are not with me?
Nowhere! Because You are ALWAYS with me!
If I could fly away to the farthest part of the earth,
Your presence would still surround me.
You hold me in the palm of Your hand,
Ever watching over me, tenderly caring for me.
I am Yours forever, Lord.
Nothing can ever separate me from Your love!

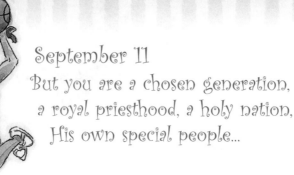

September 11

But you are a chosen generation,
a royal priesthood, a holy nation,
His own special people...

1 Peter 2:9

I'm a member of a special generation.
God is raising up a mighty army.
I am one of his soldiers!
I am one of many special people in His great army.
I will proclaim the goodness, the greatness,
the power and the praise of my God!
I will see God's glory fill the earth!

September 12

"Blessed is the servant whom his master will find
so doing when he comes. Truly, I say to you that
he will make him ruler over all that he has."

Luke 12:43,44

Living for God is the smartest thing I will ever do!
The Creator of the universe is my personal Friend.
My life has a special purpose and plan.
God will help me with all He asks me to do.
All I have to do is obey!
If I am faithful, Jesus will give me
a position in His government when He returns.
I will be a ruler by the side of the King of kings!

October 1

I will extol You, my God, O King; and
I will bless Your name forever and ever.

Psalm 145:1

I will praise You, my God and my King!
I will praise You, Jesus, Lion of Judah!
Every day I will bless You! I will tell
of Your greatness and Your marvelous works!
I will declare the glory of Your kingdom to the world!
Yours is the kingdom and the power and the glory forever!

October 2

"For I have given you an example, that
you should do as I have done to you."

John 13:15,17

Jesus is my example! He taught how to be truly happy!
Real happiness comes from giving up myself for others.
I can do the things that Jesus did.
I have God's love in my heart! His power is in me!
I can pray for the sick, lift up the brokenhearted
and show the captives of Satan how to be free!
I know true happiness because I'm a doer of God's Word.

October 3

And where the Spirit of the Lord is,
there is liberty.

2 Corinthians 3:17

I am free from the pressures of the world!
Jesus has made me free, so I can choose how to live!
I CHOOSE peace and joy and love to rule my life!
I CHOOSE to live in God's light!
No chains of the world shall bind me!
I am free to enjoy the fullness of the Lord!

October 4

...bearing with one another, and forgiving one
another, if anyone has a complaint against another...

Colossians 3:13

I won't let people upset me!
Things that others do will not make me complain.
I'll just forgive and keep smiling.
That's what Jesus does!
When I live in forgiveness,
God's peace can rule in my heart!
His peace overcomes all circumstances!

October 5

For where envy and self-seeking exist,
confusion and every evil thing will be there.

James 3:16

Strife is a work of the devil.
Being selfish leads to arguments.
Wanting my own way leads to anger.
I make up my mind not to let strife in my heart.
I resist the devil's work!
I am loving. I think of others more than myself.
I won't play the devil's game!
By walking in love I'm already the winner!

October 6

The Lord upholds all who fall, and
raises up all those who are bowed down.

Psalm 145:14

When someone sins, the Lord is right there
to take them by the hand, help them up and forgive them.
They only need to ask. No one needs to be afraid.
God is a gentle Father Who just wants to show His love.
So many people don't know God's tenderness.
I can help them to know.

October 7

Who Himself bore our sins in
His own body on the tree, that we,
having died to sins, might live for
righteousness—by whose stripes you were healed.

Jesus bore my sins on the cross.
The Bible says He also took my pains and my sicknesses.
Adam's sin brought sickness, pain, sorrow and death.
Jesus restored life, health and joy!
By Jesus' death I will live forever!
By His stripes I am healed! Instead of sorrow
I have joy unspeakable! Thank You, Jesus!

October 8

"Take heed, watch and pray; for you
do not know when the time is."

Mark 13:33

Jesus is coming back to earth soon!
He's coming to take HIS people back to heaven!
Lord, I pray for the people who don't know You yet.
Send ministers to take the gospel to all people.
Use our nation to send Your Word into all the earth.
Keep me busy doing Your work, Lord.
I won't be loafing when You return!

October 9

Rejoicing in hope, patient in tribulation,
continuing steadfastly in prayer.

Romans 12:12

Father, sometimes the news on TV is scary.
Bad things seem to happen all the time, everywhere.
My hope is in You, Lord.
I put my trust totally in You and Your goodness.
I will pray, pray, pray for others and for myself.
Your peace will fill me and give me courage.
I am not afraid.
You have a plan for the earth, and You are in control!

October 10

Because you have made the Lord your habitation,
No evil shall befall you, nor shall any plague
come near your dwelling.

Psalm 91:9,10

Lord, You are always with me. I will never let You go!
I walk with You and talk with You. We are friends.
I believe Your Word that says, "No evil shall befall me!"
No weapon formed against me shall prosper!
I am Your property! You keep me safe from harm!

October 11

...a man is valued by what others say of him.

284

Proverbs 27:21

People always watch each other.
They talk about what they see!
My life will cause good conversations!
I am not selfish or rude. I am thoughtful and helpful.
My actions show others I care about them.
My goal is to let others see Jesus in me!

October 12

Be kindly affectionate to one another with brotherly love, in honor giving preference to one another.

285

Romans 12:10

It doesn't matter who has the biggest cookie!
Having the front row seat is not important!
What matters is: Do I think of others as much as myself?
Am I showing those around me
the kindness God wants me to show?
When I treat others like Jesus would treat them
I feel really happy inside. God is happy, too.

And He said to them, "I saw Satan fall like lightning from heaven. Behold, I give you the authority to trample on serpents and scorpions, and over all the power of the enemy, and nothing shall by any means hurt you."

Luke 10:18,19; Isaiah 14:12-14

I know how to take care of the devil!
God already threw him out of heaven!
And Jesus defeated him on earth!
Then Jesus gave me His power and authority!
The devil doesn't tell me what to do.
I tell him what to do!
I bind his work in the name of Jesus!
I pray in the Holy Spirit!
I praise and worship Jesus with my whole heart!
The devil can't stay around me!

October 14
Choose for yourselves this day
whom you will serve. But as for me
and my house, we will serve the Lord.

Joshua 24:15

My mind is made up! Jesus is the One I serve! Every day I look for ways to please Him. I choose friends who love the Lord. When I'm ready to get married, God will have someone for me who loves Him! My household will have joy, goodness and peace because we serve the Lord of lords!

October 15
"And blessed is he who is not
offended because of Me."

Matthew 11:6

I'm not ashamed of Jesus!
I'll stand up for Him even when others reject Him.
I'll pray for the ones who need to change their minds.
One day they will know the truth.
When they realize their life is a failure,
I'll lead them to the One who makes my life a joy!

October 16   289

Let not mercy and truth forsake you; bind them around
your neck, write them on the tablet of your heart, and
so find favor and high esteem in the sight of God and man.

Proverbs 3:3,4

I walk in mercy and truth. Mercy means I love all
people, no matter who they are or what they've done.
They will see that Jesus loves them, through me.
I am truthful. People can believe whatever I say.
Because I show God's mercy and truth, God is pleased,
and I find favor in the sight of God and man.

October 17   290

For You, Lord, are good, and ready to forgive, and
abundant in mercy to all those who call upon You.

Psalm 86:5

Whenever I'm in trouble, I run to my heavenly Father!
He's always waiting to receive me with arms open wide!
My Father's love reaches me no matter where I am.
He is full of mercy and forgiveness.
His love never quits!
There is none as wonderful as my Lord!

October 18

Therefore I exhort first of all that supplications, prayers, intercessions, and giving of thanks be made for all men, for kings and all who are in authority.

1 Timothy 2:1,2

Heavenly Father, in the name of Jesus,
give President _____ Your wisdom and guidance.
Surround him with good counselors,
men and women with godly advice to help him.
Protect our president and our nation.
Keep us in Your light, so that we may surely be
one nation under God. Amen.

October 19

...I wish you were cold or hot.

Revelation 3:15

I'm a Christian, and I want the world to know it!
I want everyone to know the risen Lord as I do!
I'm excited about serving the King of kings!
My energy is dedicated to Jesus!
I won't grow cold or lazy. My fire won't go out!
Jesus is coming soon, and I'll be ready!

October 20

A faithful man will abound with blessings.

Proverbs 28:20

I am someone people can depend on.
If Mom or Dad asks me to do a job, I do it.
I don't forget! I don't put it off until later!
I am faithful in my schoolwork.
I do my daily assignments without being reminded.
Because I am dependable, I am blessed!

October 21

One's life does not consist in the abundance of the things he possesses. But seek the kingdom of God, and all these things shall be added to you.

Luke 12:15,31

My life is more than food, clothes, toys and vacations.
God gives me plenty of good things because He loves me.
I don't need to worry about getting more and more.
I spend my time doing good in the world around me.
The things I have here on earth won't last long.
But the good I do in Jesus' name will last forever!

October 22

There shall not be found among you
anyone who practices witchcraft, or
a soothsayer, or one who interprets omens, or
a sorcerer, or one who coiffures spells...for all
who do these things are an abomination to the Lord.

Deuteronomy 18:10-12

I will guard my soul. God's Word warns me that witchcraft,
magic and fortune telling are tools of the devil. They
are DANGEROUS. These things deceive God's people
and lure them into Satan's territory. I resist them!
I resist any influence of magic, witchcraft or fortune
telling that has ever come upon any of my ancestors!
I am redeemed by the blood of Jesus Christ!
I am full of the power of the Holy Spirit!
Satan can't touch me, in Jesus' name!

October 23

I can do all things through Christ
who strengthens me.

Philippians 4:13

Jesus said He would help me to do anything!
I CAN be a good student with His help.
I CAN learn to read with good understanding.
I CAN think and reason and put thoughts together.
I CAN do number work with ease.
I CAN be good at whatever I set my mind to do!
All things are easy for Jesus, and He's my coach!

October 24   297

Therefore, as the elect of God, holy and beloved, put
on tender mercies, kindness, humbleness of mind, meekness,
longsuffering; But above all these things put on love...

Colossians 3:12,14

I am God's child.
I am loved and valued by my heavenly Father.
Because I AM God's child, I ACT like God's child.
I have the nature of Jesus.
I am full of mercy and kindness.
I am gentle and patient in all my ways.
Above all, I walk in the love of Jesus for all people!

October 25   298

Let no one deceive you with empty words, for because
of these things the wrath of God comes upon the sons
of disobedience. Therefore do not be partakers with them.

Ephesians 5:6,7

I let the Word of God guide me.
I don't listen to suggestions from the devil!
I won't listen to bad ideas that may come from my schoolmates.
Some kids do wrong things because they don't live for Jesus.
I know right from wrong! The Holy Spirit helps me
listen to God and do what is right.

October 26

Blessed is he who considers the poor;
the Lord will deliver him in time of trouble.

Psalm 41:1

299

Jesus has a special love for the poor.
He wants me to remember them, too, and help
them. God has blessed me so I can bless others!
When I share what I have, I spread God's love.
I make God happy, and He pours more blessings on me!
He delivers me in time of trouble! He protects
me, so I can show the world His goodness!

October 27

For even when we were with you, we commanded
you this: If anyone will not work, neither shall he eat.

2 Thessalonians 3:10

300

I'm not afraid to work! Work can be a blessing!
Work helps me grow up into a useful, happy person.
Work doesn't have to be boring; it can be fun!
I will keep a cheerful attitude!
There are lots of things I can do to help at home.
I'll work hard in school, too! I will be
a valuable person: to myself, to others and to God!

October 28

Do you not know that friendship
with the world is enmity with God?

James 4:4

My Friend, Jesus, is all goodness and light and love.
In Him are all the true treasures I will ever need.
The things of the world do not offer me much.
The world is full of sin, pain and sorrow.
I choose to be friends with Jesus and not with the world!
I set my heart to follow the things of God.
He gives me real joy! He never lets me down!

October 29

"The thief does not come except to steal, and to kill,
and to destroy. I have come that they may have life,
and that they may have it more abundantly."

John 10:10

The devil is a thief! He tries to rob God's people!
Jesus is the Good Shepherd. He protects and blesses!
The devil lies. Jesus tells the truth!
The devil gives sorrow. Jesus gives joy!
The devil makes people sick. Jesus heals!
The devil steals. Jesus provides all of our needs!
The devil is all bad. Jesus is all good!
I'M GLAD I BELONG TO JESUS!

October 30

He who keeps you will not slumber.
The Lord is your keeper. The Lord
shall preserve you from all evil.

Psalm 121:3b,5a,7a

Heavenly Father,
You never go to sleep! You're always watching over me!
I can lie down and go to sleep in peace.
I have no worries or fears. Because I know
You won't let anything bad happen to me.
My confidence is in You!
Daytime and nighttime, I trust in You!

October 31

This is the way you shall bless the children of Israel.

Numbers 6:28 (24-26 personalized)

The Lord is my God. I am His child.
The Lord will bless me and keep me;
the Lord will make His face shine upon me;
the Lord will be gracious unto me;
the Lord will lift up His countenance upon me,
and give me peace, now and forevermore.

Deuteronomy 10:12-30 (Personalized)

My reason for living is to love and serve God.
I respect and honor my God.
I walk in His ways.
I love Him with all my heart and all my soul!
I keep His commandments.
For the Lord my God is the one great God.
He is mighty and awesome!
He is just and full of mercy!
I will hold fast to Him with all my strength!

November 2

And He said to them,
"Take heed what you hear..."

306

Mark 4:24

I pay attention to what God tells me!
I think about His Word day and night.
I will live the way He instructs me, so my life
will be prosperous and happy!
The more I USE God's Word, the more opportunities
He will give me to use it!
With His Word working through me,
I can change the world around me!

November 3

Do not grumble against one another, brethren...

307

James 5:9

I'm not a grumbler!
Complaining is for the birds!
I am happy and cheerful!
People are glad when they see me coming,
because I share the joy that's in my heart!
I'm not a grouchy grump! I'm a pleasant praiser!
Hallelujah!

November 4   308

For He shall give His angels charge over you, to keep
you in all your ways. They shall bear you up in their hands,
lest you dash your foot against a stone.

                                            Psalm 91:11,12

Thank You, Father, for Your angels guarding me!
I will confess Your Word, Lord, because the
angels listen for and act on Your Word.
I will be obedient, so I don't tie the angels' hands;
I will try hard to listen to You and to my parents.
I will be confident in You!
I receive Your protection day and night! Amen!

November 5   309

Honor your father and your mother,
that your days may be long upon the land
which the Lord your God is giving you.

                                            Exodus 20:12

When I obey my parents, I am obeying God.
I am always happiest when I obey!
When I'm listening to Mom and Dad,
I am walking in God's will. God can protect me!
He can keep me safe and give me long life.
Thank You, Lord, for Your power helping
me to obey. I am blessed, and I'm a blessing!

November 6

"Therefore, whatever you want men to do to you, do also to them, for this is the Law and the Prophets."

Matthew 7:12

I treat others like I want them to treat me.
I don't push or shove. I wait for my turn.
I'm not a tattletale. I am a peacemaker.
I am not greedy. I share.
I enjoy giving more than receiving!
By walking in Jesus' love, I'm truly happy.
Others know I really care about them,
and God can work in their hearts, too!

November 7

There is one who scatters, yet increases more...
The generous soul will be made rich, and he who waters will also be watered himself.

Proverbs 11:24,25

I can never lose anything by giving!
If I give something away, the Lord gives me more!
I am sensitive to the needs of others.
I have joy in sharing with those who don't have enough.
I can give my prayers, my money, my toys or my clothes.
I will never lack any good thing!
Because I remember others, God remembers me!

November 8
312

Let the word of Christ dwell in you richly in all wisdom,
teaching and admonishing one another in psalms and hymns
and spiritual songs, singing with grace in your hearts to the Lord.

Colossians 3:16

I am rich because I have God's Word! His words are
treasures I will hold onto all my life!
Because of the Word of God in me, I am
a blessing to others! I encourage them!
I share the wonder of God's love and power.
I am happy that God can use me!
I will sing songs of praise to Him forever!

November 9
313

Trust in the Lord with all your heart, and lean
not on your own understanding; in all your ways
acknowledge Him, and He shall direct your paths.

Proverbs 3:5,6

I trust in the Lord with all my heart. Even when I
don't understand everything going on around me,
I know I can depend on God. He's my heavenly Father!
Jesus is my Friend! The Holy Spirit is my Helper!
The Lord will guide me all the days of my life.
I will grow up into His perfect will!

November 10

Now I urge you, brethren, note those who cause divisions and offenses, contrary to the doctrine which you learned, and avoid them.

Romans 16:17

Lord Jesus, I may have just a few friends,
but they'll be friends who love You!
I can love all people, but I can't always follow their example.
Lead me to godly friends, Lord.
Thank You for putting good influences in my life.

November 11

Now, therefore, you are no longer strangers and foreigners, but fellow citizens with the saints and members of the household of God.

Ephesians 2:19

I'm a citizen of two countries! I am a citizen
of the United States of America (or other nation);
but eternally and forever I'm a citizen of heaven!
I am a member of God's family.
All the other saints who have ever lived
are my brothers and sisters! We're ALL
citizens of heaven! We'll have the biggest celebration
in the universe when we all get together with Jesus!

November 12

...and being fully convinced that what He had promised He was also able to perform.

Romans 4:21

316

Because of Jesus, I'm just like Abraham!
God gave Abraham a promise that seemed impossible. But Abraham believed God! He and Sarah received the promise.
I believe God gave promises so He could make them happen.
All the promises in the Bible are for people like me.
God will perform His Word when I believe and speak it;
The faith He gives me will bring it to pass in His timing.

November 13

For this cause everyone who is godly shall pray to You in a time when You may be found; surely in a flood of great waters they shall not come near him.

Psalm 32:6a

317

I pray to You alone, Lord. You always hear me.
When trouble seems to be all around,
it will not overtake me.
You are my hiding place. You keep me safe.
You surround me with Your presence. I am full of hope
and courage. Nothing can steal my joy.
The God of my salvation will never let me down.

November 14

It is impossible for God to lie. He who promised is faithful.

Hebrews 6:18,10:23b

318

When God's Word says something, it's true! God can't lie!
When God says He will love me forever, I believe Him.
I KNOW I AM LOVED!
When God says He will provide for all my needs,
I say, "MY NEEDS ARE MET!"
When God says I am redeemed from sickness, I say,
"THANK YOU, JESUS, I AM HEALED!"
My faith is in God, because He is faithful!

November 15

Their sins and their lawless deeds I will remember no more.

Hebrews 8:12

319

There are two things God can't do: God can't lie AND, God can't remember our sins after we have repented and said, "I'm sorry." I can depend on God's Word because it is true. God wants to DO only good FOR us! And He wants to SEE only the good IN us! So He gives us promises that He remembers! And He forgets anything bad that would come between us!

November 16
320

Where there is no wood, the fire goes out;
and where there is no talebearer, strife ceases.

Proverbs 26:20

I am not a talebearer! I don't tattle or gossip!
If I see a person doing something dangerous,
I will let someone know to protect their safety.
But I'll use my words for good and not harm.
Telling bad news does no good to anyone.
I will bring good reports of good news!
I look for the good things in all people!

November 17
321

Brethren, if a man is overtaken in any trespass, you
who are spiritual restore such a one in a spirit of
gentleness, considering yourself lest you also be tempted.

Galatians 6:1

When I see someone sin, I'll remember that God loves them.
If it's someone I know, I will try to talk to them.
I'll tell them in a gentle way that God loves them,
but He doesn't love their sin.
If they listen and repent, I'll rejoice!
If they don't listen, I will pray for them.

November 18

Do not associate with those given to change; for their calamity will rise suddenly.

Proverbs 24:21,22

322

I will choose my friends wisely. Some people serve God
for a little while and then they serve the devil.
They keep changing their minds! I have made up my mind!
I'm going all the way with God!
I'll pick friends who feel the same way I do!

November 19

If it is possible, as much as depends on you,
live peaceably with all men.

Romans 12:18

323

I resist the spirit of anger in the name of Jesus!
I refuse to let strife into my heart!
When strife comes in, joy and peace go out...
I won't let that happen! I'll forgive quickly,
even when the other person is wrong.
I'll be so full of peace and joy that
others can't even get angry around me!
Thank You, Jesus, for victory over strife!

November 20

As each one has received a gift, minister
it to one another (and) let him do it
as with the ability which God supplies.

1 Peter 4:8-11

324

God supplies all my abilities. He gives me the ability to
learn in school. He gives me special talents in music, art,
sports or other things. He gives me qualities from His
Spirit like love and compassion. He puts His words into
my mouth so I can minister hope to others. For all that
God gives me I am thankful. Help me, dear Lord, to use
my gifts and abilities to bring glory to Your name!

November 21

But be doers of the word, and not
hearers only, deceiving yourselves.

James 1:22

325

I love to hear God's Word!
The Word of God refreshes me! It guides me.
It tells me what to do to be happy.
It tells me how to make others happy!
I'm not just a listener to God's Word...
I'm a DOER of the instructions He gives me!
I'm a tool that God can use to help change the world!

November 22

And we urge you, brethren, to recognize those who labor among you, and are over you in the Lord and admonish you, and to esteem them very highly in love for their work's sake.

1 Thessalonians 5:12,13

326

Thank You, Jesus, for my pastor. Thank You
for teachers who watch over me and train me.
I love my pastor, Lord; and I pray for Your
power and grace to fill him.
I love my teachers. May Your will be
done through each one of them.
Thank You for my parents, too, Lord.
Protect them and fill them with
Your wisdom, Your joy, Your health
and Your strength. In Jesus' name.
Amen.

November 23

Instead you ought to say, "If the Lord wills, we shall live and do this or that." But now you boast in your arrogance. All such boasting is evil.

James 4:15,16

Lord, I place all my plans and desires in Your hands.
I ask Your advice concerning all I want to do.
I don't brag about things my family and I do, the things we buy or the plans we have.
I am willing to say, "Your will be done," in all things.
May all that concerns us bring glory to Your name.

November 24

And if you are Christ's, then you are Abraham's seed, and heirs according to the promise.

Galatians 3:29

I belong to Jesus Christ, the Son of the living God!
I am redeemed from the rulership of sin.
I am redeemed from sickness.
I am redeemed from being poor.
Because I belong to Jesus, my life is blessed!
No curse can come on me! I live an abundant life!
All my needs are met for my spirit, soul and body!

November 25

329

He who is faithful in what is
least is faithful also in much and he who is
unjust in what is least is unjust also in much.

Luke 16:10

I'm faithful. I do the little jobs Mom and Dad
ask me to. I keep on working until I finish.
I do my best in school. I am dependable.
God is watching me! When He sees I am faithful in all
of these things, He will know He can trust me.
Then He will give me greater jobs to do for Him!

November 26

330

For God is not unjust to forget your work and
labor of love which you have shown toward His name,
in that you have ministered to the saints, and do minister.

Hebrews 6:10

God sees me all the time.
He smiles whenever I'm a blessing to someone.
If I give my money for the gospel, God knows.
If I pray for God's people in need, He hears.
If I treat other people with kindness, He sees.
All the good things I do are pleasing to God.
I don't do good things to be noticed by people.
I do them to please my heavenly Father!

For we do not wrestle against flesh and blood,
but against principalities, against powers,
against the rulers of the darkness of this age,
against spiritual hosts of wickedness in the heavenly places.

Ephesians 6:12

When I get mad, I get mad at the devil!
The trouble is not with my friends or family.
The devil is the real troublemaker!
He tries to get people upset, mad or angry.
People's faith can't work when they're
in strife...so the devil loves strife!
But I'm on to his tricks! In the mighty
name of Jesus, I bind that troublemaker!
With God's wisdom and grace in me,
I have victory over strife!

November 28

But it is good to be zealous in a good thing always, and not only when I am present with you.

Galatians 4:18

I'm excited about Jesus!
I love living for God!
My life is happy because I know who I am!
I know I have a special purpose.
God needs me!
I am super abundantly energized to
live every day all the way for Jesus!

November 29

Train up a child in the way he should go and when he is old he will not depart from it.

Proverbs 22:6

I am being trained by my parents.
I'm learning how to live a godly life.
I'm learning to walk in faith and love and victory.
I will never leave the Lord! I will never depart from God's Word!
I will seek the kingdom of God first,
now and always!

November 30
And he who wins souls is wise.

Proverbs 11:30b

God says whoever wins souls is wise.
When I tell someone Jesus can help them,
I'm planting good seeds in their soul.
God can use every word I share in love.
He can cause those seeds to grow!
God has a special reward for soulwinners:

Those who are wise shall shine
Like the brightness of the firmament,
And those who turn many to righteousness
Like the stars forever and ever.

Daniel 12:3

December 1
Ephesians 3:14-19 (Personalized)

I bow my knees to the Father of our Lord Jesus Christ, from whom the whole family in heaven and earth is named, that He would grant me, (child's name), to be strengthened with might through His Spirit in my inner man, that Christ may dwell in my heart through faith; that I, (child's name), may be rooted and grounded in love; that I may be able to comprehend with all the saints what is the width and length and depth and height and to know the love of Christ which passes knowledge, and that I may be filled with all the fullness of God. Amen.

December 2
A wise son makes a glad father.

Proverbs 10:1

Thank You, Lord, for filling me with godly wisdom.
With Your wisdom working in me, I will bring forth
good fruit. My life will bring honor to Your name!
The light You put in me shines on all those around me.
My thoughts, words and actions make my parents happy!

December 3

If you extend your soul to the hungry and satisfy
the afflicted soul, then your light shall dawn in the
darkness, and your darkness shall be as the noonday,
The Lord will guide you continually, and satisfy
your soul in drought, and strengthen your bones;
you shall be like a watered garden, and like
a spring of water, whose waters do not fail.

Isaiah 58:10,11

I have compassion on the poor.
I pray for the needy, and I give to help them.
I do my part to feed the hungry and homeless.
God is able to love others and meet
THEIR needs through ME.
Because I am willing, God meets my needs.
He guides my life into paths of joy.
He strengthens my body.
I am like a watered garden.
I will never dry up!
I will never have any lack
because my heart is extended to others.

December 4

Yes, I think it is right, as long as I am in this tent to stir you up by reminding you, knowing that shortly I must put off my tent, just as our Lord Jesus Christ showed me.

2 Peter 1:13,14

Peter was Jesus' disciple.
When Peter had finished his work for Jesus and was old,
he knew he would die soon. He was not afraid to die.
He said that dying was like stepping out of a tent.
The tent represented his earthly body.
When Peter died, the REAL Peter (his spirit)
stepped out of his body just like he had walked out of a tent.
He went right to heaven!
He didn't mind leaving the old tent (his body) behind,
because Jesus had a new body for Him.
When you belong to Jesus, you don't have to
be afraid to die! Because you go right from
this earth to your new home in heaven!

December 5　　　　　　　　　　　　　　

For what is our hope, or joy, or crown of rejoicing?
Is it not even you in the presence of our
Lord Jesus Christ at His coming?

                           1 Thessalonians 2:19

My HOPE is to live a life totally for Jesus.
My JOY is in knowing the King of the universe
as my personal Friend and Savior!
My JOB is to share Him with the world.
My CROWN will be seeing people in heaven
who are there because
I showed them the love of Jesus!

December 6　　　　　　　　　　　　　　

Continue earnestly in prayer, being
vigilant in it with thanksgiving.

                           Colossians 4:2

I am faithful in prayer!
I pray daily for my family, for my pastor,
for our nation and for the world.
I intercede for others when God leads me to.
He needs someone who will be obedient and pray
when there's a need for supernatural action!
My prayers can help put God's power on the spot!

December 7

"Are not five sparrows sold for two copper coins? And not one of them is forgotten before God. But the very hairs of your head are all numbered. Do not fear therefore; you are of more value than many sparrows."

Luke 12:6,7

God loves me so much that He
knows how many hairs are on my head!
He loved me before I was even born.
He will never put me aside!
He will never forget me!
His love is greater than the ocean and
wider than the sky!
There are no words that can
tell how much God really loves me!
I will always be able to trust in His love,
because He will never, never leave me!

December 8   342

Praise the Lord! Sing to the Lord a new song,
and His praise in the congregation of saints.

Psalm 149:1

I will sing to the Lord a new song!
I'll make up songs of praise from my heart!
I'll sing to Him as I lie in bed!
I am joyful in the presence of my God!
For He loves me, and He is pleased with me!

December 9   343

That the sharing of your faith may become effective
by the acknowledgment of every good thing
which is in you in Christ Jesus.

Philemon 6

My faith is effective! Jesus lives in me!
His power and authority have been given to me!
I am full of His compassion. I'm led by His Spirit.
Every good thing has been given to me so I can
walk by faith and help others walk by faith!
My faith brings good results in my life.
As I share my faith, there will
be good results in many people's lives!

December 10
Now may the God of peace Himself
sanctify you completely; and may your
whole spirit, soul, and body be preserved blameless
at the coming of our Lord Jesus Christ.

1 Thessalonians 5:23,24

My spirit, soul and body belong to the Lord.
Jesus has given me power to control my actions.
His Holy Spirit lives within me and helps me.
The devil is my enemy. But Jesus is my Friend!
Jesus has already defeated the enemy!
Jesus in me makes me happy, strong, and able
to live a victorious life!
I will guard my spirit, my soul and my body
so Jesus can keep working through me
to bring honor to my heavenly Father!

December 11

For there are three who bear witness in heaven:
the Father, the Word, and the Holy Spirit;
and these three are one.

1 John 5:7

Father, I am a three-part person, and You are, too!
You are God the Father, God the Son and God the
Holy Spirit. I love You, Father God. I am Your child.
I love You, Jesus. You are my big Brother.
I love You, Holy Spirit. You give me comfort and help.
Thank You, Lord, for giving Yourself to me
in so many wonderful ways!

December 12

Whom having not seen you love. Though now
you do not see Him, yet believing, you rejoice
with joy inexpressible and full of glory.

1 Peter 1:8

I haven't seen Jesus like His disciples did.
But I don't have to see Jesus to believe in Him!
His Spirit lives in me! I can feel His love and
His presence all the time! He never leaves me!
I'm bubbling with joy because Jesus is real to me!

December 13

Repay no one evil for evil.

Romans 12:17

347

Father, sometimes kids have said things that hurt me.
There have been those that have hit me or thrown something at me.
I forgive them, Lord. Even if bad things like that
happen again, I will still forgive.
I won't say ugly things back. That doesn't help.
I won't get anyone into trouble. I'll just try
to act like Jesus. And Jesus will work it all out!

December 14

Let no one despise your youth, but be an example to the believers in word, in conduct, in love, in spirit, in faith, in purity.

1 Timothy 4:12

348

I'm not too little for God to use me!
I'm young, but I'm mighty! I am serious about
living a life worthy of my Lord and Savior.
I am an example of God's love. I am obedient.
I show good conduct wherever I go.
Faith is working in me. I have a pure heart.
Even though I'm young, my life is
an encouragement to others!

December 15 349

And we know that all things work together
for good to those who love God, to those
who are the called according to His purpose.

Romans 8:28

God caused me to be born at the right time and place!
He put me in this world for a purpose!
He made sure I had the equipment I need!
The Bible teaches me! Jesus is in me! The Holy
Spirit gives me power to do God's work.
I believe that all of the gifts God has
given me are working together for GOOD! I am
working together with God to change the world!

December 16 350

You are of God, little children, and have overcome them,
because He who is in you is greater than he who is in the world.

1 John 4:4

I am God's property! Jesus lives in me!
Jesus is greater than the devil, who is in the world.
Nothing the devil might try to bring against me can be greater than Jesus!
So I am not going to be defeated! I am an overcomer!
Greater is He who is in me than he who is in the world!

December 17

Let your conduct be without covetousness,
and be content with such things as you have.

351

Hebrews 13:5a

Jesus is the most valuable possession I have.
He is my greatest treasure! My heart does not envy
people who are richer than I am. I don't worry about
kids who have more toys or bigger houses than I do.
I am content! I am thankful for every blessing
that God and my parents give me. I will always
remember: Jesus is the greatest gift of all—
because He gave me Himself!

December 18

By this we know love, because He laid down
His life for us. And we also ought to lay
down our lives for the brethren.

352

1 John 3:16,17

Jesus left His home in heaven and came to earth for me.
He left the riches and glory and beauty there,
to walk the dusty roads of earth and tell of God's love.
He was the Creator of life, Who laid down His life for me.
Jesus really loves me.
I will give up my life too, for Jesus.
I'll give it up by living for others and not myself.
I'll give my time, my love, my prayers, my money.
God's kingdom will be larger because I give.

For everyone to whom much is given, from him much will be required; and to whom much has been committed, of him they will ask the more.

Luke 12:48b

I am very blessed!
I have been given much.
I have God's Word in me as a child.
I have grown-ups who love me and are training me, and
I have God's Holy Spirit and power inside of me.
Because I have so many gifts, God expects a lot of me!
He needs me to be a faithful servant.
He needs my life—all I do and say—
to be an example of His love to the world.
I will walk in God's faith and love and power!
I will use the gifts He has given me for His kingdom!
I will be a blessing to this generation!

December 20

354

Note: These next Scripture-confessions are written in such a way as to minister to the child's natural curiosity about heaven, and also to impart the "revelation blessing" which God promises to those who read and hear this powerful prophetic book.

Blessed is he who reads and those who hear the words of this prophecy, and keep those things which are written in it; for the time is near.

Revelation 1:3

I'm getting ready to be supernaturally blessed! I'm learning God's prophecies in Revelation! God tells all about His big plans for heaven and earth! I'll be hearing His words and putting them into my heart. My life will be full of grace and peace, because I know what God's going to be doing! One day soon, I will see Jesus reigning as King of kings and Lord of lords. There will be peace and beauty and joy in His kingdom FOREVER!

December 21

...and there was a rainbow around the throne, in appearance like an emerald. And from the throne proceeded lightnings, thunderings, and voices.

Revelation 4:3,5

After Jesus takes all of us Christians up to heaven, I'll see GOD'S THRONE!
The beauty of His throne will be breathtaking!
Around it will be a rainbow. Lightning and thunder and power will come from the throne. Thousands of angels will be everywhere! Everyone will be shouting praises and rejoicing to be in the presence of God!

December 22

The city was pure gold, like clear glass. And the foundations of the wall of the city were adorned with all kinds of precious stones...And the twelve gates were twelve pearls...And the street of the city was pure gold.

Revelation 21:18b,19a,21

I will see the Holy City of God!
My mansion will be there! God's city will be more beautiful than anything I've seen here on earth!
The city is made of pure, solid gold. It is surrounded by a wall made of beautiful jewels!
The streets are solid gold and clear as glass!
The twelve gates are made of twelve GIANT pearls!
The only way through the gates is by knowing Jesus.

December 23

And the city had no need of the sun or of the moon to shine in it, for the glory of God illuminated it, and the Lamb is its light.

Revelation 21:23

Heaven is brighter than the sun!
The glory of God and the light of Jesus
are so bright there's no need for the sun!
There is no night in heaven.
No one will get tired or need to go to sleep.
I'll never get bored! There are plenty of exciting
things to do to keep me busy!

December 24

And God will wipe away every tear from their eyes; there shall be no more death, nor sorrow, nor crying; and there shall be no more pain, for the former things have passed away.

Revelation 21:4

No one ever gets hurt in heaven!
No one ever gets sick or dies!
Because NO EVIL can ever get into heaven!
No one will ever cry or feel sad.
If anyone has been sad on earth,
God will wipe away all their tears.
He will fill everyone up with laughter!
We will be running and leaping with joy!

December 25

So also is the resurrection of the dead. The body is
sown in corruption, it is raised in incorruption...
We know that when He is revealed, we shall be
like Him, for we shall see Him as He is.

1 Corinthians 15:42; 1 John 3:2

Everyone who goes to heaven will get a new body!
We will still look like ourselves, but we'll have
a young, healthy, strong body like Jesus!
If anyone was crippled on earth, they will be able
to run and jump and play in heaven!
If anyone has lost an arm or leg on earth, they
will have brand new arms and legs in heaven!
Everyone will be totally whole and healthy forever!

Thank You, Jesus, for leaving heaven long enough to come to earth and give
all of us a chance to become God's children. Thank You for all the wondrous things
You have prepared in heaven for those who love You! Happy Birthday, Jesus!

December 26

Then I saw heaven opened, and behold, a white horse. And He who sat on him was called Faithful and True...

Revelation 19:11

I will see Jesus sitting tall and majestic on His beautiful white horse! I will see the glory of His countenance and the gleaming crowns on His head! He will be the one Ruler of heaven and earth! He will judge all nations. He will rule in righteousness. There will be peace and brotherhood in the earth! Everything in heaven and earth will be the way God wanted it to be from the beginning!

December 27

And the devil, who deceived them, was cast into the lake of fire and brimstone where the beast and the false prophet are. And they will be tormented day and night forever and ever.

Revelation 20:10

The devil's days are numbered! After Jesus returns, He's going to finish Satan off! He will throw him and all his followers into a lake of fire forever! The devil will never bother anybody again! Jesus will be King of kings and Lord of lords! His majesty and His glory will fill all of creation!

SUBJECT INDEX

SUBJECT INDEX

SUBJECT INDEX

SUBJECT INDEX

Prayer of Salvation

A born-again, committed relationship with God is the key to the victorious life. Jesus, the Son of God laid down His life and rose again so that we could spend eternity with Him in heaven and experience His absolute best on earth. The Bible says, ***"For God so loved the world, that he gave his only begotten Son, that whosoever believeth in him should not perish, but have everlasting life" (John 3:16).***

It is the will of God that everyone receive eternal salvation. The way to receive this salvation is to call upon the name of Jesus and confess Him as your Lord. The Bible says, ***"That if thou shalt confess with thy mouth the Lord Jesus, and shalt believe in thine heart that God hath raised him from the dead, thou shalt be saved. For whosoever shall call upon the name of the Lord shall be saved" (Romans 10:9-10,13).***

Jesus has given salvation, healing and countless benefits to all who call upon His name. These benefits can be yours if you receive Him into your heart by praying this prayer:

Heavenly Father, I come to You admitting that I am a sinner. Right now, I choose to turn away from sin, and I ask You to cleanse me of all unrighteousness. I believe that Your Son, Jesus died on the cross to take away my sins. I also believe that He rose again from the dead so that I might be justified and made righteous through faith in Him. I call upon the name of Jesus Christ to be the Savior and Lord of my life. Jesus, I choose to follow You, and ask that You fill me with the power of the Holy Spirit. I declare that right now, I am a born-again child of God. I am free from sin, and full of the righteousness of God. I am saved in Jesus' name, Amen.

If you have prayed this prayer to receive Jesus Christ as your Savior, or if this book has changed your life, we would like to hear from you. Please write us at:

Harrison House Publishers
P.O. Box 35035
Tulsa, Oklahoma 74153

You can also visit us on the web at
www.harrisonhouse.com

The Harrison House Vision

Proclaiming the truth and the power
Of the Gospel of Jesus Christ
With excellence;
Challenging Christians to
Live victoriously,
Grow spiritually,
Know God intimately.